FORGET the CORPORATE BOLLOCKS!

How to Get Rid of Stress at Work, Deal with
Job Layoffs, and Come Out Happier than Before

CAMILLE WORDSWORTH, MBA

BALBOA.PRESS
A DIVISION OF HAY HOUSE

Balboa Press books may be ordered through booksellers or by contacting:

Balboa Press
A Division of Hay House
1663 Liberty Drive
Bloomington, IN 47403
www.balboapress.com
844-682-1282

Print information available on the last page.

ISBN: 978-1-9822-6931-9 (sc)
ISBN: 978-1-9822-6933-3 (hc)
ISBN: 978-1-9822-6932-6 (e)

Library of Congress Control Number: 2021910324

Balboa Press rev. date: 05/19/2021

FORGET THE CORPORATE BOLLOCKS!

CAMILLE WORDSWORTH spent most of her career as an analyst in the fields of marketing and finance. She has lived in the United States, the Caribbean, and Europe; consequently, she has a deep affinity to the plight of global workers. In this latest book, Camille shares her own personal experiences and challenges as a corporate employee.

This book is dedicated to those who refuse to believe that . . .

1. Myth: *After a certain age, you become too old to follow your dreams*

TRUTH: You are NEVER too old to become the person you dreamed of becoming. The minute you decide to become that person and start living and acting in that way, you are whoever you say you are. Why choose to live in the shadows when you were made for greatness? Release fear from your life and just let it go!

2. Myth: For you to win, someone must lose

TRUTH: The world is enhanced when we let our light shine. There is limitless abundance and prosperity in the world. There is enough wealth for every human being and then some.

We can all prosper without taking from each other by doing what we love and what brings us the greatest joy. When you are successful, the entire world revels in your success, because you are now able to enrich the lives of others through your services or products. The world is waiting to be enriched by your talents!

3. Myth: You need to have money to make money

TRUTH: You only need to have an idea that is commercially viable. Then you need to nourish and believe in your idea, keep it safe, and believe in yourself. Stand by your dream until it comes true. The forces and people you need to bring it to fruition will show up. When the student is ready, the master will make an appearance.

4. Myth: You are helpless to change the world

TRUTH: The smallest of actions help to fill the universe with hope. Think of a butterfly that has such tender wings, yet it sets up an explosion of growth and rebirth through the tiniest movements of its wings. Sometimes all it takes is a kind word to make rainfall on a thirsty soul.

The actions of each person when combined with others create an avalanche that will not be denied by anything or anyone in the physical world. We can make a difference if we do our bit for our planet and for those around us. In every moment we have an opportunity to change the course of the world by simply changing our own lives.

CONTENTS

INTRODUCTION

I use the phrase "corporate bollocks" to refer to the oppressive organisational cultures I have experienced in my work life in both the private and public sectors. Corporations that facilitate unethical corporate cultures are responsible for abusing their employees and brazenly depleting our global natural resources.

There is a colossal failure in consumer trust because many corporations refuse to act responsibly and truthfully. Many corporations intentionally destroy our planet through their blatant disregard for environmental legislation. For example, in 2015, Volkswagen's (VW) executive team admitted that over eleven million diesel cars worldwide had been fitted with devices aimed at rigging pollution emissions test readings.[1] What is even more shocking is that VW acknowledged that they were aware of the existence of these devices in the United States. So not only were these US cars emitting up to forty times the allowed levels of nitrogen oxide pollutants into our environment, VW was responsible! We are all affected by the increased pollution. Unfortunately, the short termism, which drives decision-making in many global companies, is destroying our planet and our livelihoods.[2]

Another incidence of corporate negligence is the John West tuna scandal. The British tuna supplier was exposed for its unsustainable fishing methods. John West had promised not to use fishing devices that drew in endangered shark and turtle species. However, it was discovered that they had gone back on this promise. According to a report in the *Guardian*, "John West is using the fish aggregation devices in its fishing

---

[1] Russell Hutten, "Volkswagen: The scandal explained," *Business reporter, BBC News*, October 7, 2015, http://www.bbc.co.uk/news/business-34324772.
[2] Edmund S. Phelps, "Short-termism Is Undermining America," New *Perspectives Quarterly*, 27, no. 4, October 28, 2010, 17–19.

fleet despite a promise in 2011 that 100% of its tuna would be sustainable by 2016."[3]

This book exposes the path to ending the destruction of our livelihoods, our families, and our planet. There is a way to regain our personal power before we are transplanted by artificially intelligent replicas: collective consumerism (see chapter 10). Together we can remove these dehumanising organisational cultures and rebalance the scales of capitalism to our advantage.

In many countries, the victims of corporate injustice are required to provide the burden of proof, but ironically, the information needed to prove their case is held by the very corporates they are challenging. This unbalance allows many corporate managers to get away with treating their employees with indifference. Many corporate employees are subject to daily abuse by emotionally defective managers and draconian work policies. Toxic work situations can cause widespread psychological anguish and varied stress-related illness.

Many senior managers would have you believe that you are helpless, that you cannot do any better, and that you must not leave the hamster wheel. I hope this book sparks something inside of you to pick yourself up and to once again reach for your dreams. Be careful of whom you choose to place on pedestals. You might find that your true heroes are much closer to home than you might have expected.

---

[3] Press Association, "John West accused of breaking tuna pledge to end 'destructive' fishing methods," *The Guardian*, October 6, 2015, http://www.theguardian.com/environment/2015/oct/06/john-west-accused-of-breaking-tuna-pledge-to-end-destructive-fishing-methods.

CHAPTER 1

Work as We Know It

When we are no longer able to change a situation,
we are challenged to change ourselves.

Viktor E. Frankl,
Man's Search for Meaning

The world of business is rapidly becoming more complex. In the last ten years, more technology has been introduced than in the previous century. This rapid pace of knowledge, technology, and competition has forced companies to reinvent themselves multiple times, while human beings have stayed relatively the same in terms of capability and endurance. People work in corporates for many reasons; however, the vast majority of us work to earn a living to support our family and our lifestyles.

In today's corporate work environment, most employees are treated as expendables: sucked dry of their life energies and then discarded. There is little time for family life and exercise. Our work/life balance is fading, as we work longer hours to gain that illusive sense of job security. Unfortunately, there are some very unscrupulous people running many of the corporations you work for. Don't believe for a moment that they would worry about your livelihood should it come in the way of their profitability. The capital markets cheer when you get laid off or are made redundant. A company's stock price rises when you are put out of work or replaced by machines.

Many companies are under increasing pressure to conquer this new environment and to continually increase shareholder returns. However, most employees are without the right tools and support. Many employees find themselves having to cope with increased workloads shared among a decreasing workforce. Consequently, most managers are unable to extract the productivity and creativity required from their workforce.

While working for a certain organisation, my workload was quadrupled without any additional resources. It was at a time when the company was adversely affected by the 2007 financial collapse. Regardless of this economic climate, my team and I were forced to find ways to cut our spending and improve profitability. We were burdened with massive profitability targets, of which we had no input. Yet it was expected that we hit these targets without ever being told how to achieve it. We had no reason why we should continue apart from the threat of job losses.

My team and I worked tirelessly, even on weekends, to meet these targets. Ironically, after all of the sacrificed hours with our families for the sake of work, when we actually achieved the target against all odds, my entire department was still closed. We all suffered job losses. I wondered if we ever had a chance of winning. I wondered if the target was artificially set high so that we would never conceivably achieve it.

Perhaps, it was all orchestrated, so that senior management could justify getting rid of us. No matter how this scenario played out, we were destined to lose our jobs. This was just another eye-opener in a series of work encounters that led me to the realisation that working for corporates was a baited trap.

Just like a rat who spots the cheese in the metal trap and immediately runs toward it without any thought for the dangers involved, so too was our behaviour as employees. We trusted openly, we expected to be rewarded with the cheese for our hard work, but all we got was abuse, the death of our livelihoods, and being overworked.

These types of painful work experiences drove me to strive to always be in control of my work environment. I decided to never run headlong into any opportunity without first understanding the rewards and the dangers. I advise you to do the same. It is essential that when you sacrifice your time with your loved ones, your exercise routine, or your mental health, you need to be certain that you are doing it for the right reasons.

My team and I had worked so hard to keep our jobs, but in the end, we lost it anyway. Don't run blindly into that trap. Return a fair day's work for a fair day's wage to your corporate masters. Guard your time wisely and harness your creativity to dream up the life you deserve to have.

Build and work consistently until you achieve that life, and never allow the corporations to suck all of your life energy. Keep some energy, courage, and self-confidence in reserve for the accomplishment of your goals and desires.

> *Everything can be taken from a man but one thing: the last of human freedoms—to choose one's attitude in any given set of circumstances, to choose one's own way.*
> *Viktor E. Frankl,*
> *Man's Search for Meaning*

Controlling your work destiny requires conscious decision-making. You will work because this is the way you choose to earn the money to do the things that make you feel alive. You will work, but you know your limitations when it comes to how much you can produce in any given day. You will work for corporates, but you are also aware that at any given time there are abundant opportunities out there to make the money you desire.

YOUR CREATIVITY IS A KEY ASSET

Corporations will never survive without your creativity. Sometimes we offer ourselves too cheaply. We accept minimal payment for what is our most magnificent asset—our minds! We need to learn to understand how truly valuable we are before we start offering our labour to corporations.

We need to protect our ability to be creative by finding time to recover and to relax. We need to protect our abilities to generate new ideas and solutions for our lives. Your creativity is priceless to corporates but it is of even greater importance to your enjoyment of your life on this planet. It is through your creativity that you find alternative ways to earn a living, if you so desire.

Your creativity is essential to helping develop products and services that provide corporations with competitive advantages. By providing services and products that anticipate what customers need, corporates can ensure their survival in rapidly changing and highly competitive markets.

This creativity can only come from the workforce; it cannot come from robots or artificial intelligence. Human beings are essential contributors, so corporations need to start taking care of their human capital—YOU—if they expect you to produce the creativity necessary for future profitability and sustainability.

Unfortunately, most managers turn to bullying and other demoralising methods to demand creativity from their human capital. Most corporate employees are familiar with these sinister work situations, but they are often too fearful to speak about it. However, internalising these unacceptable work situations often results in stress-related illnesses, such as (1) debilitating physical pain (i.e., headaches, anxiety attacks, sleep deprivation); (2) mental harm (i.e., loss of self-confidence, guilt, anger, and depression); and (3) high employee absenteeism and turnover.

There is continual pressure from senior management for employees to produce more with less. This is a very costly problem for all involved: companies, workers, families, etc. These unrealistic demands result in a decline in productivity and create mental anguish for employees. Ironically, as the need for more trained staff grows, companies have continually cut budgets for training and personal development.

CORPORATE TIME STEALING

Many corporates are guilty of time stealing which can lead to mental exhaustion. They use technology to demand unceasing productivity from employees day and night. Time is our greatest asset and our worst enemy. When we work in such complex, highly politicised work organisations, we can easily lose sight of who we really are. It becomes commonplace to value our humanity by the titles we hold or the amount of income we can earn.

Work titles become a measuring stick from which to judge ourselves and those around us. This power hierarchy is encouraged because it keeps you suspended in fear, and, consequently, more compliant to accepting poor treatment. In the deepest sense, you adopt the mentality of a "worker bee." A "worker bee" is someone who works under the force of fear. Worker bees are prone to working extra hours because they fear losing their livelihood, as opposed to willingly offering their services. You might discover that you are either a worker bee or at risk of becoming a worker bee.

THE RISE OF THE WORKER BEE

Worker bees often include those who will do anything to climb up the corporate ladder; those who toil endlessly hoping for job security; and those who work with no direction mapped out for their future. I was a worker bee for many years. I was obsessed with proving my worth to my company. I wanted to squelch the feeling inside of me that said I was never good enough, that I was an imposter. Finally, I got sick of all the negativity in my head. I decided that I was worth my pay, that I was valuable, and I took control of my work destiny.

Nothing changed physically, but I made a mental leap. Your fears about not having a job, losing everything, feeling like a loser, is all in your mind. I have been there and back many times. Trust me when I tell you that what doesn't kill you will surely make you stronger.

I can confidently say that if you drop me anywhere in the world today, I will find a way to survive. I am no longer afraid to just let go! I know that abundance is everywhere and it is incredibly easy to make money from any commercial enterprise that solves a problem and provides a workable solution.

I am not suggesting that you should walk out on your job, but I am pleading with you to work on making that mental shift. Learn and practice visualisation, affirmations, whatever it takes to make you believe that you are enough in this very moment. Once you start believing in yourself, the world becomes your oyster.

Just remember, we all become worker bees if we view and approach our jobs as a necessity rather than a choice. Choose to believe in you. I believe that it is within you to make your dreams happen!

AN ISSUE OF TRUST

An honest man's word is as good as his bond.
Miguel de Cervantes Saavedra
El quijote

In the old days, your word was your bond. Today, there is very little trust between employers and employees. What minimal trust remains is often extinguished during company takeovers, layoffs, delayering, etc. This lack of trust leads to unsupportive and oppressive corporate cultures. It creates a stressful environment that is manifested in high work absenteeism and other stress-related illnesses.

Trust is a key ingredient in any relationship. It is the foundation from which true contribution grows. If you happen to work in a toxic corporate environment, you need to accept that you cannot trust your employer to look out for your health and your wellbeing. It is now your responsibility to look out for yourself and not to rely on your employer to provide for your future needs.

THE ILLUSION OF JOB SECURITY

In today's global economy there is truly no real job security. It is rare for an employee to be able to count on working for one employer for his or her entire career.

IT IS OKAY TO BELIEVE IN YOURSELF!

In my work life, I had many people who refused to become friends with me. They seemed to somehow recognise that I was different. It is common for worker bees to disassociate from those they believe are radicals or free thinkers in the work environment. They hedge their hopes on keeping their senior management team content while management spins their particular brand of toxic, power politics. Worker bees are often shocked when they are unapologetically kicked out of the business. They become filled with indignation and resentment for having their loyalty repaid in this way.

Worker bees who crave job security believe that if they put in the hours they will have career longevity. They tend to keep their head down and ignore the injustice around them. They are careful about what they say so as never to cause offence. Some worker bees may even support false claims against innocent employees just to keep their own jobs.

I have personally experienced this! I have had managers sit across from me and blatantly spit lies at my face in the presence of others. I don't deal in lies, so I just responded with my quiet truth. I also knew in that moment that it was time to make a change. Many corporate managers try to convince you that if you walk away, it means that you've failed in your ability to perform your role effectively. Don't fall into this trap. If your job is killing you, then its time you find another way to make a living!

When you focus on the wrong door, you fall prey to this self-defeating thinking. When you buy into the idea that you are only valuable based on other's estimation of you, then you lose your personal power and sense of grounding.

Don't miss out by focusing on the wrong door!

In 2009, there was a sad example, in my opinion, of a man who used wealth to forge his sense of significance and value. German billionaire, Adolf Merckle, committed suicide at the age of seventy-four. Merckle had been listed as one of the wealthiest men in the world.[4] His empire included a vast consortium of businesses, from pharmaceuticals to cement.

Unfortunately, a few poor business decisions had put his company into debt, and he was forced to ask the banks for a funding solution. Ironically, Merckle was so afraid of losing his reputation that he committed suicide just before the loan was approved to save his companies.

Merckle was so fearful and worried about what others would think of him that he felt his only escape was in death. He was so focused on the wrong door, what he had lost, that he failed to realise he was still sitting on more money than most people would ever earn in their lifetime.[5]

The point is whether you're rich or poor, you will always get the short end of the stick if you base your life's significance on material wealth. You will only find emptiness by focusing on the wrong door. Wealth is great, but it is certainly of no consequence to your family when you are no longer alive to share it with them. Your family values your time, attention, and love much more than any monetary pleasure you could afford them.

I think Merckle's choice to end his life was selfish. His actions affected many lives—his family, his friends, and his employees. Instead of thinking of the greater good, he only thought of himself. Learning to live for something greater than you creates your legacy and contributes to the betterment of mankind. If you live life this way, you will never worry should you lose everything you own.

Losing everything is not as important as finding the will to start again to rebuild. You see, once you have achieved it once, it is far easier and faster to do it again the second time around. You know the terrain, you

---

[4] Gordon Rayner, "Adolf Merckle: what made this German billionaire commit suicide?" *The Telegraph*, last modified January 9, 2009, http://www.telegraph.co.uk/finance/recession/4210246/Adolf-Merckle-what-made-this-German-billionaire-commit-suicide.html.
[5] Ibid.

know the path, you know what it takes, so you can achieve even more success the second time around!

Many unethical corporate managers rely on this type of inbred fear, the type of fear that led Merckle to commit suicide. Many of us are just too busy working long hours to see the writing on the wall. It is only after corporates have achieved their purpose and then discarded you when you realise how much of your life's energy was wasted on just spinning your wheels to no avail.

This is why it is imperative to have a clear distinction between you as a human being and you as an employee. Most corporates offer no brownie points for being a good parent, friend, caregiver to parents and relatives, or as a symbol of harmony and charity in your community. When we allow corporate titles and power to cloud our vision for our lives, we become worker bees.

As worker bees, we work out of fear and this is why we become stuck. You cannot rely on corporate managers to discover what you are good at; you need to find that out for yourself. Then you should negotiate for the salary you're worth. You need to set up the game of your life and make your own rules.

CHAPTER 2

Defining Employee Roles: Sheep, Wolves in Sheep's Clothing, Lions, and Lionhearts

No matter how hard the past,
you can always begin again.
Buddhist Proverb

Recognising the role you play in corporate culture is important. This knowledge is the key to breaking free from becoming a corporate pawn. We all take on roles in life. No matter how old you are, you will always adopt the role of a child when dealing with your parents. Over time, we learn to communicate our desires to our parents in a respectful way, but we will always remain their children.

Fortunately, we can break the yolk of unethical corporations because they are only temporary parents. In fact, I consider these corporations to be reluctant parents who do not wish to accept the burden of parenting. It is not necessarily wrong to wish to be supported by your company. The issue is that complete dependence on corporates for your livelihood makes you vulnerable to the fallout from senior management's poor decision-making. This desire takes away your personal power to control your work destiny, because you become addicted to the security of receiving a pay cheque.

Giving corporations power over your livelihood allows them to discard you when you are no longer valuable to them. Evolution is the only way to survive the corporate jungle. In the corporate jungle, there are four main roles we can adopt: sheep, wolves (wolves in sheep's clothing), lions, and lionhearts.

The choices we make in the corporate jungle determine whether we become wolves, sheep, or lions. Observe what role you play and make that adjustment to become a lionheart; it is your ultimate survival tool.

THE OBEDIENT SHEEP

Sheep are dutiful; they genuinely work for the betterment of their company.

They start work in good faith, and they are the last to abandon the corporate ship, even when things get tough at work. They genuinely love their work and always try to make valuable contributions.

The sheep usually occupy the lower rungs of the corporate ladder and are in abundant supply. Organisations need sheep; they need loyal followers. However, in times of turmoil, the sheep are often the first to get laid off. Since sheep can be easily replaced, they are of little consequence to corporates. Corporates often ignore sheep complaints about anti-family HR policies, work-induced stresses, and dysfunctional managerial behaviours.

In spite of this, sheep possess a kind spirit and genuinely care about others and their organisation. The problem is that sheep have come to depend on the security of a salary. They have planned their lives around their incomes because they hate having to search for new jobs. Job hunting is stressful to them. The mere thought of not knowing when they will receive their next pay cheque causes stress and panic. Sheep are afraid of the unknown and continually yearn for job security.

Another weakness of the sheep is their naivety to the power politics around them. This lack of political shrewdness makes them vulnerable to the wolves. Sheep are so busy trying to perform at their best that they fail to recognise the danger around them. When a sheep is bullied, mistreated, or made redundant by their corporate masters, they take it rather personally. Instead of seeing the big picture, sheep look inwardly and initially blame themselves for their misfortune. Their perception of what has occurred becomes a source of great mental anguish and depression. It is not uncommon to see sheep cry when confronted with courses of action they felt were unfair and undeserved.

Having spent most of my working life as a sheep, I can admit to shedding many tears when things did not work out. I experienced first-hand how truly powerless sheep are.

For many years, I would always do contract work in-between jobs. I love contract work because I'm in and out, and I don't stay long enough to get involved in office politics, or so I thought!

I had been a contractor for an engineering company for about seven months. My contract as an analyst was ongoing and extendable. As time passed, I developed friendships with my co-workers, a mixture of contractors and permanent staff. My boss was also very kind and supportive. Well, that was until I saw the CEO of my contracting firm storming out of my boss's office.

As a sheep, I obediently went back to work, happily toiling away. I had witnessed something, but it had made no great impression on me. The weeks following that day were a nightmare. My boss became mean and aggressive toward me. In the past, I could make mistakes or ask for help, but now I was being yelled at and openly chastised for simple errors, such as not putting in a total line in a report, or if he didn't approve of the colour of my PowerPoint presentation. At lunchtime, my co-workers and I would usually go to lunch together, but my boss would openly make it known that he preferred not to go if I was going.

My fellow sheep, sensing something was wrong, began to question me on what had happened between my boss and me. I had no clue! They seemed to think it was something other than work related. Some sheep even rumoured that it might have been a work affair that went awry. Those who know me never believed such nonsense.

After about two months of my boss's outward disdain for my work and my presence, I finally built up the courage to confront him about it. Well, that was a big mistake. I don't know what I expected when I entered his office, but I certainly was not expecting the reaction I got!

As I took my seat and explained the reason for my visit, I noticed my boss becoming visibly vexed. Before I could finish my third sentence, my boss interrupted me. He waved his arms and yelled at the top of his lungs. I was shocked by his reaction. I noticed his secretary and the other employees anxiously peering into the office. This was a train wreck.

My boss told me that I was ungrateful because he allowed me to stay on even when my contracting firm tried to screw him over. He ranted about the CEO of the contracting company being a crook who used his connections to place unqualified people in senior roles. I just didn't know what all of this had to do with me.

After about five minutes of his unreasonable and inappropriate display of aggression, I decided I had had enough. I got up, looked at him defiantly, and walked out of his office. I went to my desk and began packing my things. My body was overheating and my cheeks were flushing. I was so angry, I was shaking.

I hurriedly packed my things as my co-workers looked on helplessly. No one came to my cubicle to see if I was okay. I think they were all too afraid to do so. I was a bit disappointed by this, as I thought I had made some good friends. I tried not to focus on the lack of support because I was about to burst into tears.

I used all the strength I could muster to walk out of the building with my head held high, but inside I was dying. I was a ball of nerves and confusion. I kept thinking what I did wrong. Why did this happen to me? I just could not figure it out. I sat in my car and cried.

Suddenly, I heard a knock on the car window. I looked up and saw a very worried and kind face. It was my boss's secretary; she had come to check on me. She asked me what I had done to make the boss so angry. I immediately replied, "Nothing!"

She seemed unconvinced. "I have worked for him for over five years, and I have never seen him behave like that. You must have done something," she said.

I clearly understood why she was there. She was there to defend her boss, and she did not care about me. I forced a smile, started my car, and waved good-bye.

I immediately drove over to the contracting company's office. When I walked in, the receptionist sensed my urgency and told me to go into the CEO's office. Maybe she had already heard what had happened at my job. As I walked into the CEO's office, he smiled apologetically at me and offered me a seat. The CEO observed me for a few seconds before speaking. He told me that he had received a phone call from my boss just before I had arrived. He said he was sorry that I had gotten caught in the crossfire.

Apparently, the CEO of my contracting firm and my boss had been butting heads for a while over switching to a new staffing supply firm. The CEO said that it was rumoured that my boss wanted his friend, who had recently set up a contracting firm, to provide all contractors moving forward. Consequently, my boss refused to renew all pre-existing contractors. The CEO had been in negotiations with my boss to split the supply contract between the two firms, but things had gotten heated and threats were made. I had been one of the last remaining contractors at that firm.

The CEO said that my boss had been very appreciative of my work up until the business of switching to a new contracting firm. Apparently, my boss had said I would lose my job if the CEO continued to create controversy over the matter. The CEO did not take the threat seriously, because I still had some months until the next renewal date.

This was the reason why my boss purposely began a campaign to sabotage my employment. He wanted to drive me to the point of leaving. He had achieved his goal that day.

The harsh reality was that I was just an ignorant, powerless sheep. I paid no attention that day when the CEO of my contracting company stormed out of my boss's office. I was unaware of how the politics of others could hurt my career and my livelihood. I learned that you must be aware of clues in your environment so you will never be caught by surprise.

Like my example, most sheep are surprised when they get to the chopping block. However, when a sheep is kicked out of the business, they gather their belongings and quietly exit. The sheep then retreats to a place of safety until their next job comes along. Remarkably, the sheep does not bring the baggage of the past; they approach their new role with genuine excitement and perform at their best.

The sheep likes the safety of the herd. They work hard to feel that sense of security. One of the sheep's strengths is their ability to work behind the scenes. The sheep will try to rebalance the scales of justice in a creative and collaborative way. Sheep move around, helping others almost invisibly; they are keen to divert attention from themselves. Sheep choose their battles wisely and never rush into disagreements.

A troublesome problem for sheep is that they never learn from negative work experiences. They live in hope that they will be safe if they keep their heads down and do a good job. This is never really the case. No matter what sheep do they will always be a few inches away from the chopping block.

By the time the sheep wakes up to the cyclical nature of their work reality, it is often too late. Many sheep may have suffered from ill health and are now too weak to make new plans. These sheep tend to get pushed out of the business and forced into early retirement. They spend the rest of their days steeped in regret.

To survive in the corporate jungle, the sheep needs to evolve into a lionheart. In addition to the evolution into a lionheart, the sheep must always be on the lookout for wolves. Wolves are the most dangerous predators in the corporate environment because they hold immense power over the work destinies of sheep.

THE WOLF: SOME ARE HIDDEN IN SHEEP'S CLOTHING

The wolf represents the darker side of humanity; it is the yin or negative energy. The wolf is both a product of their environment as well as their choices.

The wolf is highly intelligent. They are often the masterminds behind plans to drive profitability and increase shareholder return. This is one of the main reasons wolves get brought into corporates. Wolves often fill middle to upper management roles.

The untamed side of the wolf's personality destroys the very organisations that give them sustenance. Wolves are often attracted to and rewarded by oppressive work cultures. They are often recognised for their creativity and ability to find ways to surpass industry competitors. In power-driven, hierarchical work cultures, wolves do their best work and worst damage.

Wolves thrive on recognition and material success. A wolf's love of success is addictive. The more successful they become, the more addicted they become to winning. The problem is that wolves have loose ethical codes. So when the economy is booming, wolves ride high on a wave of admiration and success.

However, in bad economies when profitability is not an easy gain, wolves may use underhanded ways of achieving their success, such as overstating profits or understating the company's debt. When wolves step onto this side of the tracks, they become harmful to their organisations. If a wolf remains unchecked and unchallenged in their work practices, they can destroy companies and livelihoods. When these wolves go rogue, they find all kinds of ways to cheat the system.

Beware of the wolf in sheep's clothing

Wolves are natural manipulators of work situations. They sometimes pretend to be sheep when it serves their purposes. Wolves like to gain the trust of sheep and use them to do their bidding. This is how wolves harness the power of numbers to gain power and influence in the organisation.

Once the wolf has asserted its authority, it is free to do as it pleases. Unfortunately, most corporates are overrun with wolves in sheep's clothing. They are the dealmakers and the pawn-pushers. These wolves like to pretend to be sheep to take advantage of the sheep's loyalty and clan nature.

Wolves are silver-tongued and often convince sheep to relinquish their ethical position for the greater good of the company. Wolves are good at manipulating Human Resources professionals in this way. However, when they can't get HR professionals to get rid of the lions or rebellious sheep, they resort to bullying to achieve their goals. Once the wolf has amassed enough sheep support, they become key players in the power politics of the organisation. Wolves then transform their trust relationship with the sheep to one that is fear-driven.

Wolves attack without mercy in the corporate environment. Your work longevity can be easily destroyed by the wolf. They demand cult-like following and do not react kindly to dissention. When wolves feel threatened, they will do whatever it takes to maintain their job security: they will tell lies, spin plots, and sacrifice innocent sheep. You will only truly become aware of a wolf's power when you end up on the opposite side of the table.

Wolves are always focused on protecting their self-interest. They will get rid of unsupportive sheep and replace them with their own cronies. Wolves hold a singular head and tend to be pervasive in middle management. They remove any managers who refuse to back them up or challenge their coercive leadership style.

Most notable, a wolf's greatest weakness is its ego. Wolves pride themselves on being smarter than their colleagues are. It is easy to deal with wolves if you can satiate their egos. Wolves drop their guard when they think you are loyal to them. Cunning lions often use flattery to control wolves and to harness their creative talents.

A wolf's ultimate goal is to rid organisations of lions just as they begin evolving into lionhearts. Wolves know that mature lions, also known as lionhearts, can see them for who they really are. Wolves are always fearful of being called out. They tend to deal with the threat of lionhearts by continuously trying to sabotage the lion's work. They cause endless frustration to lions by blocking their strategies and making the sheep rebel. Ultimately, the lion must find a win-win compromise with the wolves if they wish to save the organisation from falling into stagnation.

Wolves are power hungry. They spend most of their work careers spinning webs of deceit. Wolves tend to be the last ones to lose their jobs; they seem able to hang on until the very end.

Wolves are detrimental to corporations because they are addicted to winning at all costs. Wolves also stifle the sheep' creativity by stealing their ideas, they hinder the lions' progress by sabotaging their information, and they serve their own self-interest in all situations. Nothing is beneath them when it comes to making money. Wolves will use bribery, lies, threats, or whatever means necessary to get what they want.

Wolves are the perpetrators of corporate fraud. Wolves in global multinational companies single-handedly create chaos in the global economy just to appease their ego's need for material success. This chaos translates to losses, economic turmoil for innocent employees, the destruction of our planet, and the depletion of our natural resources.

Wolves are the destroyers of humanity. They need to be either restrained from destroying the company or removed from company boards. The problem is that they are so well dug into the system that it is hard to get them out. Wolves are the most fearsome animals in the corporate jungle.

When wolves go rogue, there is no other alternative than to get rid of them. Rogue wolves will compromise the integrity of the company to feed their need for success and recognition. Only a lionheart, which is discussed later in this chapter, has the ability and skill to get rid of a rogue wolf. If a lionheart decides to remove a rogue wolf, they know they must be prepared for a massive battle. The wolf will never go quietly into the night. They will bring down as many others as they can before it is all over.

FIFA—an organisation overrun by rogue wolves!

The unfolding of the International Federation of Association Football (FIFA) corruption scandal provided a striking example of the havoc wolves create around the world. It is endemic of the issue facing many global organisations that fall prey to wolves.

For many years, there had been rumours that FIFA's senior team, including Sepp Blatter, encouraged a culture of "clientelism" and "corruption."[6] In 2015, the whole house collapsed when the US Department of Justice spear-headed a series of investigations into FIFA's decision-making and marketing rights allocation procedures. The Swiss soon followed with its own probe, along with other countries around the globe.

---

[6] David Goldblatt, "The Fifa fiasco proves it's time to dismantle football's edifice of corruption," *The Guardian*, May 27 2015, http://www.theguardian.com/commentisfree/2015/may/27/fifa-fiasco-football-corruption.

There were several global criminal investigations launched regarding allegations of some senior members involved in bribery, racketeering, fraud, money laundering etc. There were also questions regarding the allocation of the 2018 and 2022 World Cups to Russia and Qatar.

What is interesting is how most indicted members willingly brought out hidden skeletons about each other. Wolves never take the fall on their own; they bring down anyone who is remotely connected to them. This scenario was played out in the public arena and exposes another instance of lies and corruption perpetrated by the wolves who wield global power.

Many senior officials were named in this fiasco.[7] The moral of the story is this: Sometimes in life you may have to turn your back on lucrative positions if you suspect there are corrupt people running those organisations. It is better to walk away from the promise of wealth than to have your reputation tarnished by mere association.

Life is filled with abundant opportunities to make a living. Don't be lured by big salaries or the promises of riches when you know the foundations are rotting. Eventually, the house will come crashing down like a pack of cards. You will never be able to work in filth and remain looking squeaky clean.

Choose your friends and the companies to work for wisely. In this life, there is no substitute for honour. Don't trade honour for a few pieces of silver; it is NEVER worth it. In the end, you will only hurt yourself and those you love.

Wolves never learn this lesson until it is too late. They only repent when they are caught, and even then, some still maintain their innocence. The choices we make determine whether we become wolves or lions.

---

[7] "Following the FIFA Fiasco," *Bloomberg News, FIFA, U.S. Department of Justice documents*, July 17, 2015, http://www.bloomberg.com/graphics/2015-fifa-scandal/.

If you are a wolf who has made bad choices in the past, I dare you to turn your life around. Forgive yourself and pledge to turn over a new leaf. Work on becoming a lionheart. It is a far better way to live. Choose wisely—you only get one chance at this life!

THE LION

The lion is similar in strength and creativity to the wolf. The lion is the yang, positive energy, to the wolf's yin, negative energy. The lion represents the more enlightened side of humanity.

The lion appears to be self-confident and self-assured in the work environment; however, their Achilles' heel is a nagging sense of insecurity. Many workers may never notice this side of the lion. This insecurity causes lions to feel the need to continually prove their worth to others.

Fortunately, as the career of a lion grows from strength to strength, their insecurity dissolves and they become emotionally astute. Their successes reinforce their self-belief and their confidence builds. Mature lions evolve into lionhearts.

The lion demands loyalty from its followers. They stand out very easily from the sheep. Lions love the limelight and thrive on the attention it brings. The lion is also an advocate for justice; they are often the first to roar when things are not right. The lion can either make your life at work one of the best experiences ever, or they can make it a living hell. Lions are so driven that they expect others to have the same level of intensity. They like to work hard and play hard. Lions tend to be adventurous and take risks in and out of work.

The main downfall of the lion is its impulsiveness. The lion often roars before it thinks. Unlike the sheep, the lion is not afraid to take the lonely high road. Many lions do well in corporates until they get knocked back by wolves. It is important for lions to keep moving forward and to not believe the lies that wolves try to sell them.

Wolves know the buttons to press to get lions to doubt their abilities. If the lion is lucky, this may not happen until later in their careers, but by then they would have evolved into lionhearts. When a lion is confronted with corporates who try to treat them unfairly, they immediately lash out. The lion gets into the battle and fights until it becomes pointless to do so. The lion never goes quietly into the night with its tail between its legs.

In the downtime, the lion works on plans to become invincible. The lion learns from its negative work experiences and treats corporates with the caution they deserve. Lions thrive in loyal environments; they place a high value on trust. They will give all they have to the corporation that can develop that bond with them. The lion will bring all of its creative energies to bear for the success of the company. Committed lions will utilise their knowledge and skills to protect the business's interest. Lions have the ability to creatively solve challenges that normally cause most corporates to fail.

If a lion makes a wolf a permanent employee, the lion must remain vigilant at all times to ensure the wolf stays on the straight and narrow. As a wolf successfully grows in the organisation, their egos grow exponentially until they believe they no longer need the lion. The wolf then works to destroy the lion's reign in the organisation.

Like the sheep, the lion is also kind and cares about humanity. However, the lion also has challenges to overcome when trying to evolve into lionhearts. Lions need to choose their battles carefully when it comes to fighting wolves. Wolves can trip up unsuspecting lions by making them react impulsively to situations based on wrong information. This projects the lion in a bad light, and they lose the respect of the other animals in the organisation.

Successful wolves work relentlessly to discredit lions. To achieve this, wolves keep a tight leash on the sheep. Since the sheep are in abundance, it makes sense that those who control the masses possess the most power in the organisation. Wolves work hard to ensure that they are the taskmasters of sheep.

Even if a lion makes it to the top of the organisation, the wolves will be in control if the lion does not have the respect and loyalty of the sheep. The lion has two choices: form a mutually beneficial alliance with the wolves in return for the loyalty of the sheep, or roar loudly about the injustices and hope that the sheep will stir and come to their rescue. The latter never works, and that's another reason why wolves are so deeply entrenched in corporate life.

Lions are most vulnerable to wolves when they are transitioning to a lionheart. They are easily agitated and they sometimes move too hastily because of their need to prove their worth. Wolves tap into this weakness and lay traps with false information so lions will fail with their policies and plans for the future of the company. Lions can use wolves to inject energy and creativity into the workforce, but they should only use these talents in a consultancy type of arrangement.

When a lion gets to its full maturity, the wolves become powerless over them. Lionhearts have the gift of clarity. They can NEVER be manipulated or tricked into doing things that are in conflict with the greater good. Lionhearts create the boundaries that wolves must work within if they wish to continue to work in the organisation.

EVOLVING INTO A LIONHEART

A lionheart is essentially a combination of the emotionally intelligent lion and the heart of humanity. It is a state of being where you possess the brevity to stand up for what is right without being confrontational or aggressive. It is a path that is untainted by prejudices and ego-trips.

A lionheart is graceful and self-confident with a big dollop of humility. Lionhearts transcend their work environments. They sit outside of situations and never take any of what happens at work personally.

Lionhearts intimately know their value to the world; they never rely on outward recognition to determine that value. They know their value intimately because they spend years honing their craft and skills. Lionhearts love what they do and enjoy it because they are so great at it!

The evolution into a lionheart is critical if you want to be successful in the corporate jungle or life in general. Lions naturally progress to this state through constant effort and skill development. Similarly, sheep have to make a conscious choice to live in this space. Living as a lionheart is a state that is attainable by anyone who wishes to seek it out.

Although wolves may try to become lionhearts, it is difficult for them to fight against their addiction to winning at all costs. Eventually, if the wolf does not experience enough positive reinforcements in its new path, it will revert to working for its own self-interest.

Evolving into lionhearts holds the key to work/life balance. Lionhearts are practiced in the art of maintaining mental freedom from enslaving corporate work cultures. Although lionhearts work in good faith, they do so without endangering their health, well-being, or sacrificing well-deserved family time!

To a lionheart, life without special celebratory moments, serving others, and relaxation is just a waste of their time on Earth. Because of this belief, lionhearts make these things a priority in their lives. Interestingly, when a lionheart puts these non-negotiable demands to corporates, they accept it without challenge. Lionhearts heed the saying that no one on his or her deathbed has ever lamented, "I wished I had worked more!"

Once lionhearts become successful at delivering what has been promised to the sheep, the sheep will slowly start forming a line behind the lionheart. At this point, the lionheart and the sheep will work in harmony to get the company back to a profit-producing machine. However, because the lionheart is a lover of humanity, they will ensure that the company treats its employees well and that they replenish the natural resources they use in their production processes.

Today, there are some lionhearts running companies. You can see evidence of this through their early adoption of environmental accounting systems and their investment in clean energy sources. This is in contrast to companies run by wolves who unscrupulously destroy the livelihoods of their employees without a second thought.

Lionhearts find things that inspire them and bring them into a state of appreciation for their time here on Earth. If your life feels like a drag and you are just toiling away, then it is time to make a change. It is up to you to take action to transform your life from a lion, wolf, or sheep into a lionheart.

How does a sheep become a lionheart?

It is far easier for a sheep to become a lionheart than for a wolf to do so. In fact, I am not certain wolves can never become lionhearts unless something happens in their lives that dramatically changes them viscerally. Sheep are already good, hardworking, and possess an innate ability to care for others. This stems from their herd-like mentality. They will look out for the weakest link.

All a sheep needs is to DECIDE to become a lionheart and take positive steps in that direction. Sheep need to seize opportunities to step into the front. Sheep are used to keeping their heads down and invisibly grinding away. To become a lionheart they have to be willing to be noticed by others for their unique talents. Sheep need to learn to step outside of their comfort zones. They need to be able to walk away from the herd if they know that something is fundamentally wrong with a company's product or service.

To fully evolve into lionhearts, sheep need to become aware of their political environment. They need to learn to see people as they are and not who they expect them to be. Sheep should not become angry when others don't act as they themselves would have. They need to accept that wolves will behave according to their nature.

The main reason sheep get so easily fooled by wolves in sheep's clothing is because they expect everyone to behave ethically. Therefore, to gain the sharp insight of a lionheart, the sheep must learn to both accept the true natures of those they encounter and create strategies for managing these personalities within the corporate environment.

The sheep must be prepared to repulse any attack from the wolf by using its wits. A sheep, who outwits a wolf, by pretending to be ignorant of the wolf's plans, then secretly sabotaging those plans to protect the company, is truly a lionheart. Yes, sheep need to become a bit enterprising to rise above their station.

Then, most importantly, a sheep must teach the path to other sheep. The issue is that sheep are slow to follow and it takes a while to get them to take action. However, once a sheep DECIDES to become a lionheart, there is no stopping them. This determination is a key quality for evolving into a lionheart.

I became a lionheart far too late in my career. The years as a sheep had kept me below my true potential. It took a lot of time for me to accept how very terrible and ruthless wolves were. Today, I use that knowledge to help people find the right job and to learn how to survive in the corporate jungle so they can become successful a lot sooner. Unfortunately, I still have many friends who are stuck in energy-sucking, unrewarding jobs. This book was written to guide them out of their muddle.

In summary, consciously deciding the role that one plays in the corporate environment is the difference between whether you or the corporation controls your work destiny. It is vitally important that you understand the role you play, because you need to evolve into a lionheart. Becoming a lionheart is the key to your life's happiness and job satisfaction.

CHAPTER 3

Cultivating a Perspective of Impersonality

You already possess everything
necessary to become great.

Native American Proverb, Crow

When you accept employment from a company, you have a responsibility to provide the services you promised. In return, the company pays you for that privilege. This simplistic transaction is overshadowed with words and phrases such as "shareholder value," "company politics," and "culture."

However, the bottom line is this: a company becomes a parent when you work for them, and it is their duty to protect you from mental and physical harm during your time of employment. Sadly, in most corporates, the Human Resources department or the workers' union—the first ports of call for work-related problems—fail to protect employees from abuse because many of the senior officials are under the yolk of the corporation. They are reluctant to stand by the employees against the corporate engine that lubricates their pocket.

THE CHURN CYCLE

As an employee, it is essential that you learn about the "churn cycle." The churn cycle is the time it takes for employees to move to new roles, either externally or within a company. You cannot afford to become too complacent in any role. Unless you are continually being challenged and growing in your role, your time at the company is numbered.

It is essential to be on the lookout for warning indicators. Even if you may not have been in a role for more than five years, you may need to start moving on, even after two years. An obvious warning signal is if you observe work colleagues, who have worked incredibly hard, suddenly disappear. You look at their empty desk and you wonder what happened to them.

There might be rumours that they did something so terrible that they lost their job. Don't fall for those constructed lies! More often than not, the employees were kicked out of the business and silenced through compromise agreements. That's why there is just an empty desk and no one to speak about what actually happened.

Another warning that there is trouble in the pipeline is a year-on-year decline in profitability. You may hear other employees discussing failing profitability or departmental restructures. This is usually a good indicator that time is running short. I like to be prepared, so I would start getting my CV or résumé out the door.

The most common signal is disharmony among departmental managers. You never want to be caught in someone else's crossfire. Sometimes you will experience rifts between department heads. If you happen to work for a less powerful boss, then it might be time to move to a different department. If your boss continues to create havoc, the senior management team may decide to get rid of your entire team as retribution.

I have a friend who was constantly denied promotions in her department. If you are stuck in a role, you have performed at your best, you have learned your craft well, and you still cannot be recognised, you need to find a new role. Just hoping that things will get better will cause you to become unhappy and your work performance will suffer.

If you stay in this downward spiral, you will begin to lose your self-confidence. Eventually you will come to accept that you are not good at your job and that is why you have not been promoted. Step out of this thinking pattern. See the situation for the prison that it is. Value yourself enough to find an opportunity that celebrates your talent. Don't buy into your boss's oppressive assessment of your capabilities. They mean to keep you there. Rise up!

I once worked for a boss who had a massively high turnover. Within a few days of working for him, I found out that two of my team members were moving to other departments. During the interviewing process, it was never mentioned that I would become the only person reporting to this team leader. Within weeks, I realised why there was such a high turnover of staff in his department. My boss was a bully and he was as incompetent as he was mean. I, too, soon moved on and never looked back.

It is amazing that Human Resources never flagged or questioned why there was such a high turnover in this department. After all, recruitment is a costly business, and companies could save a lot of money if they got rid of rotten managers instead of constantly having to pay for compromise agreements to exit those wounded by these same abusive managers.

WORKPLACE BULLYING

There is a disturbing truth about many companies with regard to bullying. It is not that the Human Resources team cannot identify the instances of bullying; it is how they manage it, which is failing their employees. The perpetrators are often senior and middle managers or, rather, the wolves in sheep's clothing. These wolves are great manipulators and liars.

Sadly, I have spoken to many people from various industries and they all seem to report the same issues. This epidemic of poor management and coercive leadership is securely hidden under masks of agreeability and forward thinking. Many corporates offer lip service to the latter and continue to support the former behind closed doors.

Most middle managers respond to their employees' requests for time off with resentment. Employees' needs outside the organisation, such as family needs, relationship needs, and mind and body renewal needs, are often frowned upon. Ironically, as managers ignore these employee requests, they continually demand more time, more creativity, and more innovation from their staff.

Many HR representatives know that employees are being treated badly. Off the record, many frown at their requirement to back up managers and to shove the employee out of the door. They often observe the employee wilting under the weight of his or her manager's deceit and the organisation's failure to correct these types of coercive behaviours.

Many employees at all levels are facing this wave of bullying. The problem is getting worse, because the law lays the burden of proof on the victim. Yet, it is the company that has access to all of the pertinent case information. This effectively keeps power in the hands of the perpetrators. The meek employee then has little option but to sign compromise agreements to protect his or her health and mental faculties.

WHO WILL STAND FOR YOU?

Whenever there is trouble at work, we often find that there is no one able to help us. Everyone involved is too busy helping themselves—lawyers need to be paid; HR professionals need to support their establishment; fellow colleagues are too afraid of losing their jobs; unions want to amass more power at your expense.

The only person who is on your side is you! The truth is, when trouble comes, you often have no choice but to leave. This is not cowardice; it is just living to fight another day. You may be legally bound to not say anything negative about the company and its products; however, that does not stop you from boycotting the company or recommending superior products to your friends and family.

A CASE OF BLACKLISTING: BAD REFERENCING

Companies are quick to get you to sign compromise agreements so that you can never tell anyone about their dark secrets. In my case, my ex-boss was free to give bad referencing on my behalf, but I could not tell anyone about the issues I had encountered while working for her.

After returning to university and completing a master's degree in business and a professional accounting qualification, I reapplied at the same company for a few senior roles. I chose to apply to the same company because the roles were in a completely different department and I now had these advanced qualifications. Also, I believed that my arbitration case would have been of little consequence, since I had spent years building competence and specialising in a completely new area.

It never occurred to me that my ex-boss would be involved in providing references. The HR system apparently did not have notes regarding our arbitration, nor did the HR team even bother to match the levels of seniority.

It had been five years since I worked for that company. My ex-boss had even been demoted during that time and she was now three levels below the role I applied for. My ex-boss did not have the recent experiences, seniority, or the qualifications to provide a weighted opinion of my capability for the new role. Additionally, since we had been in arbitration, surely her opinion of me would have been biased.

It took another two years before I found out why I had not been shortlisted for any of the senior roles at that company. A head hunter from the recruitment company called to ask me about my most recent application. I told him I had not heard about the job and thought I had been blacklisted. He insisted that it was not possible and looked into his system to see the feedback I had received for my previous roles. To his surprise, the system listed that I had bad referencing and so my CV was not progressed to the interview stage on both occasions. I was furious when I heard this. Now, years later, I wonder why I had been so naïve!

I called an employment attorney to find out about my rights. Once again, I was told that I had little recourse. The company held the information I needed. So, not only had my ex-boss managed to push me out of the company, but she was now messing with my livelihood, and I could not do a darn thing about it! I imagined my references coming across my ex-boss's desk, and she would have a revengeful smile as she called HR to give them an "unbiased" and "off-the-record" reference.

Apart from my ex-boss's appalling behaviour, I was also surprised by the recruitment firm's response. They admitted they had other candidates who had mentioned not being shortlisted for one reason or another, but they were totally unprepared to do anything about it. Since the recruiter and I had known each other for a long time, he explained why they chose to do nothing.

Apparently, being an approved provider for this company involved a lot of money for the recruitment company, and they were not in a hurry to rock the boat. It did not matter to them what the reasons were for the bad referencing or whether it was fair to the candidate or not. Their main goal was to find someone the company would be willing to hire or they would not make any commission.

I was enraged and disappointed. I knew it was not the recruiter's fault; it was the influence of his senior management team. It was the decision of those who wielded power to choose money over human dignity and fair treatment. In this experience, I got a glimpse first hand into the global corruption spun by corporates.

Money is the rope that they use to tie everyone into subservience. Money is the whip many corporate managers use to punish those who dare to challenge their corrosive behaviours that hurt helpless employees. I was a victim of this system, and no one was willing to stand up with me to seek justice.

Yet could you blame the recruiter for wanting to keep his job? Could you blame him for not wanting to challenge the mighty HR department of a major global company? Wouldn't you be cowering in your boots if you had to tell your major revenue contributor that their system is flawed?

Do you see how easy it is to justify to yourself why it is okay to turn a blind eye to unethical practices? As corporate employees, we deal with unethical issues on a regular basis. Truthfully, when we are in the system, most of us choose to look away. When I told one of my close friends about my experience, she comforted me by saying, "You are better off not going back there, so just move on." This head-in-the-sand technique only keeps these corporates and its bullies free to continue to demean and cause harm to their employees.

This incident is now all water under the bridge. However, I wanted you to be aware of how dangerous wolves can be even long after you have left the company. Always ensure that you have written references from those who are willing to speak about you positively. It is becoming commonplace to leave corporates through arbitration, so you are not alone.

Just remember, not all people are the same. The world is filled with good and bad apples, and so are corporates. Unless the culture is completely rotten to its core, I would encourage you to apply for other roles at the same company.

If you have had issues with management in the past, have it noted on your new job application. If you don't, you will not get past the gatekeepers at the company. This information will enable HR to check into your work history and make a more informed decision on your application. This action will also prevent any instances of bad referencing from your former toxic boss. You would rather have your say than not have an opportunity to state your case. The fact is, you can put your head in the sand and pretend nothing happened, or you can walk fearlessly along the path.

If you bring up an issue in the past, it is not accepting blame; it is just stating what it is. By proceeding in an open and honest manner, it would show that you have nothing to be ashamed of. Don't be so naïve to think that it will not come up, it will! Deal with it head on in a matter-of-fact way.

You could include in your note something similar to this, "I worked at your company in, *include the date*. It was for a completely different role, requiring different skill sets. Unfortunately, on that occasion it did not work out due to personality incongruence with my then manager, *include their name*. When the matter was resolved, I was informed by the human resourcing representative that there would be no issue with me applying for future roles at the company. I have more recent references with regard to my work ethic and character. I would be happy to provide these should you decide to proceed with my application for the role."

CHAPTER 4

The Dark Side of Corporate Life

*The true division of humanity is between
those who live in light and those who live in darkness.*

Victor Hugo

I t is often said that we don't see people for who they really are. We super-impose our values and morality onto others, so good sees good in all, and the bad sees only that others are out to get them. This was how I came to understand how people could be so unnaturally terrible to each other at work.

DISREGARD FOR WORK/LIFE BALANCE

While working on my master's degree, my research took me to places that were quite unexpected. What happens in life is sometimes unavoidable. However, does your past make you any less significant or less capable than others? I realised that if I lived according to public "role models," I had no chance of happiness or success. While working on a piece for women in business, I discovered a couple of things.

Firstly, I discovered that there was overwhelming research supporting a man's desire to spend time with his family. Although it seemed logical, he is a human being after all, and many employers place this desire in the domain of women. Although the laws have changed to allow men to take some leave at the birth of their children, men do not usually take the time off. To most men this is a non-option, because it can become career limiting. Time off might be interpreted as a lack of commitment to the company.

Secondly, I observed propaganda spinners masquerading as helpful research foundations. For instance, a well-regarded research foundation unquestioningly suggested that the only way to make it to the top echelons of companies was to forget work/life balance.

This blatant diminishing of our need for regeneration and mental peace was quite disturbing. I realised at that moment that we were all trapped in a vicious cycle and being brainwashed to accept a pre-determined status quo.

Furthermore, we were punished with static career progression if we did not walk the proverbial line. Our freedom to live life on our terms was being destroyed with pre-defined plans made by corporates who cared little for our happiness.

Thirdly, I realised that women who chose to stay at home with their children were treated as outcasts by the corporate world. Politicians go on about harnessing the potential of stay-at-home moms, but this is only lip service. I was disturbed to hear of top women who advocated placing careers before motherhood. It was astonishing to read about the actions of top executives who openly flaunted their disregard for a healthy work/life balance.

A prominent female executive explained that the way for women to get to the top was to only have children when you had sufficiently progressed in your career. I suppose all of those women who happened to fall in love and have children without managing their career progression are doomed to a life of mediocrity!

Another top female executive displayed how a woman could manage a successful career and motherhood at the same time. It was rumoured in the press that she returned to work only two weeks after giving birth and had a nursery built next to her office so that she could breastfeed her child. While it was an incredible feat for this CEO, she is not really your everyday woman. She is a super achiever who is highly intelligent and highly paid. I doubt most men or women could follow in her footsteps; she is quite a rare breed.

Surely, if we have to be superhuman to get to the top, those board spaces will remain void of common people for years to come! More importantly, these super elite are too far removed from us and cannot truly represent the interests of the global workforce. Just look at their remuneration packages—hundreds of percentages above frontline employees' earnings.

It is our responsibility to regard all information with a certain degree of scepticism. We need to see through the illusions and find what is right for our circumstances and families. We need to live life by our rules and not some super-imposed, one-size-fits-all standards. We need to forget the corporate bollocks!

THE MYTH OF FLEXIBLE WORKING HOURS

Many employees, particularly women, have to fight to get flexible working hours such as working from home, or hours outside the 9 to 5 rule, even though many employers claim to offer it. Some employees are lured with the benefit of flexible working hours, yet it becomes a mute issue once they get into the organisation.

Other organisations use the ideal of flexible work hours to minimise the cost of employee benefits. For instance, some corporates offer their employees full time employment only if they agree to work weekends. These unsociable work hours keep most employees just below the hours required to qualify for full time benefits.

Sometimes your employer may verbally say that it complies with the legal requirements for flexibility, but in reality it is not supported by their corporate culture. I have spoken to countless employees who struggle to just work for one day at home. Ironically, most workers who work from home tend to put in more hours because they don't want their bosses to think that they are not performing. This adds another element of stress and time-stealing from employees.

The best way to make an employer grant you flexible working hours is to negotiate it into your contract. Having this in writing will help you to get the time approved more easily. However, it will not remove the cultural pressures imposed by the organisation to make you feel guilty for asking for something that was promised. In most cases, employees who desire flexible working hours end up sacrificing this need by allowing the company to dictate their work hours without challenge.

THE CURSE OF SELF-INTERESTED MANAGERS

I was always under the impression that corporates hire people who have the skills they need. Ironically, while working as an executive recruiter, I often encountered quite the opposite. Many corporate managers refuse to hire those more qualified than them. I am not sure how these managers actually help their respective businesses grow. Evidently, their actions could explain the never-ending cost cutting, layoffs, and restructures.

A failure to increase resource capability through proper talent injections results in companies with fewer employees who are managing unrealistic workloads. Lionhearts who wish to save their companies would do well to examine whether hiring practices are aligned with building capability and competitive advantage or ego-driven by wolves.

These managers are wolves in sheep's clothing, who are bent on maintaining their status quo. They exhaust their employees until they are no longer able to be productive. If they manage to squeeze any creativity from their employees, they steal these ideas and present it as their own to upper management. This inevitably causes frontline employees to keep ideas and great business solutions out of the business.

The gloves come off when profit reports are due. As the profitability of the company declines, these wolves engage in cost cutting. Sheep are sacrificed on the chopping block through a series of restructures and layoffs. No one bats an eye as stock prices soar, shareholders get the gains they are promised, and the cycle starts again. This epidemic is widespread, and this vicious cycle is destroying families and causing a multitude of work-related stresses.

Most people respond to these narcissistic, ill-equipped, and overly demanding wolves by quickly moving on without burning their bridges. While this may be a good solution for you, it does not fix the issue and the organisation begins to rot from the inside. These managers simply refuse to take responsibility for their lack of emotional intelligence and effective leadership skills.

Have you ever had a manager who was absolutely clueless? I once worked for a manager who constantly criticised my work. However, when I asked for guidance, she seemed incapable of articulating what she wanted. Considering that I was not trained to be a mind reader, I was given a series of poor performance reviews.

Ironically, in a meeting with a significant business partner, my manager presented my presentation, which she'd told me was "absolute garbage," and passed it off as her own. I could not believe my ears! I had to quickly compose myself as she repeated all of my "rubbish" ideas.

After the meeting, I raised the issue. My manager unapologetically told me that I should not expect recognition for terrible work. I had to literally pull my jaw off the floor! I felt like I was stuck in some terrible horror movie and I would be killed if I didn't escape. The lack of trust made working with this manager impossible. In the end, I chose to leave rather than put up with her lies and constantly demeaning behaviour toward me.

There is a method to dealing with energy-sucking, idea-stealing managers. It involves never directly confronting them about their behaviour. Instead, document all of your conversations; this will be the only proof you have of their actions should you choose to discuss this with HR. It is important to make plans for your stance. If you can find another role, move swiftly onwards and upwards. If not, begin to prepare for a rainy day, because you will be getting a lump sum and a compromise agreement, which can be a blessing. As I always say, never leave your hard-earned money on the table. In fact, take the money and use it to fund an amazing life!

I grew up learning to treat others as I would like to be treated. Somehow it appears that these values are now lost in the corporate work environment. When our conscience has no place in the world of work, then surely we are mere animals in a concrete jungle. Why would we not want to live by a code that promotes respect and goodwill?

Great managers are as rare as the numbers you bet on at the roulette table. A great manager is self-aware, emotionally intelligent, and competent in his/her roles. If I received a penny for every time someone told me about a bad manager who was making their working lives miserable I would be rich! Be aware! These draconian managers are simply masking their own incompetence by doing their best to sabotage your efforts to perform well.

Employee refinement!

If you don't fit neatly into designed categories, or if you expose poor management by those who are above your pay grade, you will be tossed out of the business. This is the corporate idea of "employee refinement." This activity ensures that the worker bees stay under the control of their corporate masters.

It prevents you from upsetting the apple cart by demanding more than you are getting. This "employee refinement" process also ensures that those around you will be too afraid to stand by you when you decide that this system is not working for you.

POLITICAL WARFARE

Like it or not, there is immense political warfare in many corporate work environments. Political acumen is especially needed if your organisation is highly stratified and your value is determined by your grade level. Eat or be eaten—that is the motto of the political elite, the wolves, in hierarchical work cultures. I use the word "elite" to signify the wolves' perceived stature, not that I hold them in this regard. This type of narcissistic senior management is found in oppressive corporate cultures. As usual, if left unchecked, they cause the downfall of the company.

SURVIVING THE POWER POLITICS

There are many ways to survive in a politically charged work environment, but I hope you will not choose behaviours that will deplete your humanity. Over the course of my career, I often found that the work was never the issue; it was all the politics and backstabbing that went on under the surface that caused me stress and kept me from achieving personal success.

All over the world, there are those who have mastered the art of power politics in most corporates; they are either lionhearts or wolves. Wolves are egotistical blood-sucking vamps, which are only there to promote themselves. The only way to beat them is to follow the age-old advice: "Keep your friends close and your enemies even closer."

Surviving corporate politics is hard work. It requires a lot of patience to cut through all of the bollocks you will encounter. You have to learn to recognise your enemy before you can beat them at their own game.

A wolf's justification for treating you badly is not important. You need to be able to defend yourself against their confidence-sapping attacks. If you are not careful, you will become a victim of your own ignorance. Too often we superimpose our values and morality on others; this then results in us holding our hands up in the air and lamenting on the stupidity or absurdity of the other person. We never realise that the issue is not with them; it's with us!

People are the way they are just because they have freedom of choice. By accepting this precept, you will not fall into the futile trap of trying to change others. Even more foolishly, you will not waste your time challenging people who are closed to any suggestions. To try to change these types of people would be like pounding on a wall with your bare fist and expecting the wall to crumble. The effort is futile and you should place your energies elsewhere.

By far the most evolved way to survive corporate politics is to follow the way of the lionheart. Use wolves, but don't let them rule over you. Never compromise your integrity for anyone or anything. Wolves will put a noose around your neck if you ever bend the rules, but don't bend the rules. Be fair and just in your dealings, and keep your language positive about everyone and everything. This is the only way to keep the wolves from gaining power over you.

Discipline yourself to keep your work at a high standard, as this is what will speak volumes on your behalf. Finally, whether you find joy in your work or outside of work, take time to fuel your soul. Your inner joy will shield you from indulging in petty squabbles at work. You will be bigger than your environment and beyond the reach of the wolf.

Without leverage the battle is already lost

> *Give me a lever long enough and a place to stand and I will move the earth.*
>
> -Archimedes

I worked as a part-time telephone sales person when I first started university. Like many of my fellow students, we found that this was a great way to earn some extra cash. We would go to work at 5:00 p.m. and finish our shift at 9:00 p.m.

For three hours, we would earn about $20, which would fund our beers at the local bar. I recall this really charismatic guy, Chris, who continually complained about our appalling work conditions. One major point of contention was that once you signed in for a shift, you could not leave the phones. If you had to go to the bathroom, you would be automatically deducted twenty minutes of pay; it did not matter if you took less time.

Chris finally got tired of preaching to us and decided to take some action. He created a petition outlining our desires for improved work conditions. He insisted that everyone sign the petition. However, a group of us chose not to participate. It was not that we did not agree with what was written on the petition, rather, we did not sign it because we knew it would not make any difference.

We had no leverage; we were only students, and no one cared about our petty, little job. More importantly, we made a choice to work there; we liked the hours and the money was not so bad. We could have gone elsewhere, but we chose not to. We were contented with our lot in life. There was no motivation for us to rock the boat.

After a week of insisting that everyone needed to sign, Chris finally decided it was time to make his stand. He had collected twenty signatures out of a workforce of thirty students. Chris believed that this was sufficient to present to the site manager. The site manager was very tactful and thanked Chris publicly for caring to do something for his co-workers. The site manager promised that he would raise the points with senior management, and that he was confident that things would change in the coming months.

This promise settled everyone, and it was business as usual for a while. A few days before Thanksgiving break, a memo appeared on our desks. The memo said that there was a slow-down in sales and some of the staff would be cut by the end of the shift. Well, it did not take a brain surgeon to know who would be cut. Expectedly, Chris was the first one to go. By the time we got back from Thanksgiving break, the office was re-populated with a completely new team.

The moral of this story was that sheep are powerless to change the system. You need leverage—someone with power has to care about your issue. Just putting together a petition of lowly sheep is of no value and will create no change.

Although Chris's actions were admirable, we had no leverage with upper management. Without leverage, the only possible outcome would be that we lose our jobs and not have money to spend in the pub.

The underlying lesson is that we can't expect to bring down the machine of capitalism when we are worried about replacing our incomes. I can't expect you to stand in solidarity when you live pay cheque to pay cheque.

So here is what I propose: you need to sort out your life. You can change your circumstances by controlling your spending habits. By living on less, you will not feel so burdened and tied to the corporation. You may also find that you have extra money to travel and see the amazing creatures on our planet. It is only then that you will be moved to save the rhinos from poachers, or join whatever causes needs your support. It is only by first helping ourselves to find a way out of our burdensome lives that we can then focus on helping others and our planet.

I have been to the pit and I have risen out of the ashes. I want you to have that chance to live like the few who don't dread Sunday nights. I used to hate Sundays because I was one step closer to Monday. Now, it does not matter what day of the week it is; I enjoy each day all the same. You, too, can live like this. All you have to do is choose the path that you want and work toward achieving that life. It will happen with a little effort and self-belief.

You may need to stay employed with a corporate until you set up your new life. If that is the case, you will need to be able to survive in a power-hungry culture until the time is right to declare your exit. To bide your time in corporates, you need to keep your opinions to yourself.

A politically charged environment exists only when there is trade in gossip and misdeeds. You can shut all of this down by choosing to remain neutral and choosing to stand up only for high-stake opportunities. Let the small stuff slide under the bridge. If you happen to lose your job for standing against something that would destroy your company, then you are better off leaving anyway.

CHAPTER 5

The Emerging Drone Culture

The robot is going to lose. Not by much. But when the final score is tallied, flesh and blood is going to beat the damn monster.

Adam Smith
(1723–1790)

Most corporates say they don't want an army of drone workers, yet that is exactly what they are developing. To be sustainable, corporates need to harness creativity and innovation from its human workforce. The entrepreneurism that corporates demand will never come from human shells that are too afraid to share their opinions.

Corporates continually try to find competitive advantages through artificial intelligence. Ironically, there is a cheaper and more sustainable way to do business. Corporates would win if they provided employees with the time and freedom to let their imaginations soar. This type of creativity will only occur in healthy, positive company cultures.

Corporates that truly care about developing and nurturing their human capital will be the only ones left standing in the future. Inspiration does not come under extreme stress and pressure; we have our sparks of genius in the little, restful moments of joy. By maintaining company cultures, which continuously strip away the assets of our humanness, disrupt opportunities to be charitable to colleagues, as well as sharing precious moments with our families and friends, the corporates empty us of what fuels our creative sensibilities.

Many senior management teams believe that robotic machines and computer programs are superior to humans because they can work longer hours and provide no personal issues. However, what they seemed to have overlooked is that artificial intelligence can only produce what you input, whereas the human brain is more complex with unlimited potential.

In a bid to save money, many corporates transfer jobs to places where labour cost is lower. The people who are skilled in the originating country lose their livelihoods with nothing to show for all their years of dedication to their crafts. Instead, cheaply, poorly designed products made with sub-standard materials are fed back into the system.

Again, it is obvious, that these corporates don't care what they put out for our consumption, so why should we care to give them our money? Where is the pride in workmanship? Where is the pride in production? What does a robot or an unskilled worker know of craftsmanship? Yet we buy the products, we break them, and we replace them with more junk.

I hope the next time you need to replace a material item you will at least give some thought to how it was created and by whom. Before you put your cash in and continue a cycle of destroying the livelihoods of generations of those gifted in the arts and crafts, take pause. Is that the result you really want? This is the staple of conscious consumerism. Take the time to think through our purchases and demand higher quality and standards. Just as corporates push us, we also must push back!

If you want our intellectual capital, you need to pay a FAIR price for it!

Many unscrupulous corporations try to get resources for as little money as possible. This is why many corporates are struggling to get their employees to willingly offer up their intellectual capital. Why should employees do so when their needs are blatantly ignored? Most employees know that such corporates are not truly looking out for their best interest.

It is a given that some corporates choose not to offer many of the things employees require, such as time flexibility, childcare benefits, elderly care and the like. These corporates only look after their employees if there is a high cost to the company, or if they are legislated to do so or if there is a consequent problem in the provision of labour if certain services are not provided.

There is a shortage of highly skilled labour, which is a typical example of how some corporates manipulate the global workforce by only providing help to families when it is necessary for maintaining profit. In places like China, some corporates bend over backward to get more women into the work environment when there is high demand for skilled labour. Many large multinational companies willingly pay for the care of elderly parents and provide in-house childcare to keep women at work. This flexibility is not replicated in the West where there is a surplus of skilled workers.

The issue then becomes, why do we all not get the same benefits? The answer is simply, why should they? If these unethical corporates have no incentive to provide for their employees, they don't. We as consumers and employees need to provide that incentive. Now is the time to stand up against the corporate bollocks!

CHAPTER 6

Defending Against the Corporate Bollocks

We grow great by dreams. All big men are dreamers.
They see things in the soft haze of a spring day
or in the red fire of a long winter's evening.

Some of us let these great dreams die, but others
nourish and protect them; nurse them through
bad days till they bring them to the sunshine and
light which comes always to those who sincerely
hope that their dreams will come true.

Woodrow T. Wilson
(28th President of the United States)

To live fearlessly takes immense courage. I think it is even harder to do when you have achieved a certain level of comfort. You are neither poor nor rich; you are just stuck in the middle. You have a job that is boring but pays the bills. You have a family who loves you, but who seem to require additional energy that you simply don't possess at the end of the workday. You live your life in a boring routine, but at least you know what to expect.

COMFORT MAY BE KILLING YOUR AMBITION AND DREAMS!

A few years ago I decided that my life was not moving in the direction that I had hoped for. I felt that it was too late for me to achieve the things I once dreamed of as a child. I looked around me and saw others living this mediocre life and they appeared to be happy.

I knew that I was not happy. I feigned happiness, hoping that things would get better. I was hoping that I would come to accept and appreciate the life that I had. After all, I had food, shelter, clothing, and I knew some people did not even have that. I was dissatisfied, but I could not quite put my finger on what it was that made me so unhappy.

My friends would tell me how lucky I was, but I just could not feel it. I knew that I was fortunate to have moved from the United States to England, and to have built a life that now included a husband and two bouncy boys. I was happy with them, but I still felt like something was missing. I had an amazing husband, healthy children, a nice house, and a nice car—what was wrong with me?

TEXAS TO THE RESCUE

During that period of joylessness, my aunt came to visit me in England. My aunt and I had spent a lot of time together when I lived in Texas. I had told her that I would take her around Europe whenever she chose to make the trip over. One fine summer we went traveling for a week. We had planned all the details of the trip, but every time we tried to execute the plan something prevented it from happening. We either missed our train, or there was a delay and we'd miss our connections . . . you name it, it happened!

It was just so hectic, and we never really found time to sit and relax. We frantically moved from place to place. I think we spent four hours in Paris, visited Notre Dame and the Eiffel Tower, and then we were back on the train to Vienna. It was a mad rush of a trip.

We arrived in Vienna at one in the morning and were scheduled to leave the following morning at noon. Instead of sleeping that night, we went to a nightclub and partied until the wee hours of the morning. It was both exhilarating and exhausting. Needless to say, there was not much juice left in the tank after a hectic night out! But after only two hours of sleep, we were up and racing off to Monte Carlo.

While most people would think it was a dreadful trip, it was almost the mirror of my life. I had spent my life moving at lightning speed from one place to the next. I never quite settled down in one place for too long, at least, never long enough to develop meaningful connections and friendships.

You see, I was afraid. I was afraid that if I had stayed too long, I would become like the people around me. I was afraid that if I settled too long, I too would become stuck. This trip was what I needed to once again ensure that I was reaching for higher standards for my life.

I was so busy doing the parent thing that I had left no time for myself. In addition to this lack of time to just be, I was sucked into the comfort of my circumstances. This minimal level of comfort created a smoke screen that stood between me and my dreams. I knew my life was not the way I had envisioned it, but I was too afraid to take the leap. I was too afraid to leave the security of my life, to see what else was out there in the big, wide world. After all, I had worked so hard to get here and I became afraid to lose it all.

I was too afraid to dream, to risk, to hope. I often justified to myself that since I had lived so much of my life already and nothing amazing happened, I just needed to accept that maybe this was all there was. I am guessing you have moments when you feel that you should change your path, but like me, you were too afraid to cast your fears to the wind and step out into the unknown. I lived like this for many years. I like to call it "lost in suburbia." I became lost; I had forgotten who I was. I had given up on my dreams. I was just comfortable!

I know we all get stuck at one point or another in our lives. However, what I have learned is that you can overcome the fear that keeps you stuck. I learned to do it by never allowing myself to settle for less than I can be. I achieved a life that moved beyond fear because I would no longer accept what was unchallenging and boring to me. I wanted to live a life filled with joy, material wealth, and excitement.

THE LIES WE TELL OURSELVES

True job and life satisfaction can only be won when we are honest about who we are. When we get there, we can now begin to plot a new course for our lives. Hopefully, it will be something you have always dreamed of doing. Life is not only about achieving wealth.

I used to be afraid that if I cut off from the wealth I had acquired, I would be robbing my children of their future. After all, they need to go to college and they will need stuff along the way. I thought it would be selfish of me to cast it all to the wind and invest in myself. My time was over; this was their time now. I could never have been so wrong!

I was lying to myself, because I was too afraid to live my dreams. It had nothing to do with my kid's future. My children are energised, and they are happier than they have ever been because I am happy. As a family, we have never been happier, and it was all because I got fed up with pretending to be happy with my mediocre life and did something about it.

The truth is, to live your life passionately and with confidence is the greatest lesson you can give to your children. In that choice, they will see your courage manifested in living colour. They will learn first-hand what it is to be fearless in the face of any adversity. They will see a new hero far greater than any in the movies or on YouTube. The joy you will feel from your newfound freedom will spread and enrich your family. Yes, you may downsize or take a pay cut to follow your dreams, but what else is there?

Money is only one part of the equation. The irony is that only when you live in truth and honour your talents, will the abundance of the universe come flowing in. I don't tell you this lightly; I am not irresponsible. I tell you this because it is a truth I discovered for myself.

I can promise that the love and passion that you will have for your chosen vocation will shine in the world so brightly, and you will have more than you initially gave up. It is not a blind promise. Life rewards those who have the courage to push past their fears and to live the life they have always dreamed of living.

RE-WIRING YOUR LIFE FOR SUCCESS

You can cut the cords that bind you to your job right now by bringing your finances under control. Debt is the worse taskmaster of all.

Find alternative ways to supplement your income. The more passive income sources you create, the faster you will remove the yolk of your corporate oppressor. There are many programs that provide guidance on how to create passive income, but there are no quick, get-rich schemes.

Any time you wish to increase your income, you need to earn money. Don't be fooled by people enticing you with schemes that will make you rich in a few months. Building wealth takes time and discipline. It also requires that you become a student of wealth and learn from those who have achieved the wealth you desire.

The most important lesson I have learned about wealth is that if you build it well, they will come! You will have unlimited wealth if you provide an outstanding product or service based on something you love. You must infuse energy and love into whatever you offer to the world. Only then will you discover the true path to your financial freedom.

Have you ever eaten a dish and it was so tasty that just remembering the experience makes your mouth water? My dad is one of the best cooks I know. I love eating his food. I believe that his food nourishes those who eat it because he cooks it with such passion and love.

My dad spends hours thinking about food and what he will cook. He loves making food people enjoy. He takes pleasure in watching people eat his food, even strangers. Anyone who stops by the house while he is cooking is offered a place at his table. My dad loves feeding people and they in turn appreciate him for it.

That is the type of dedication you need to produce an outstanding service or product. Put all of your energy, passion, and love in what you put out for others to consume. By doing this, you will be rewarded with unlimited wealth and abundance. People will know that you cared about them enough to take the time to produce something amazing just for them. They will thank you by offering you their money.

When you love what you do, everything becomes effortless. This is your true path to financial freedom, time freedom, and a life filled with happiness.

FINDING THE KEY TO HAPPINESS

On my return from my trip with my aunt, I stepped out of my life and took a moment for myself. For one month, I spent the entire time figuring out how to achieve the type of life I desired. After weeks of working on my inner self, I finally realised that I had never addressed the FEAR inside of me.

My life was externally driven. I was only happy when great things happened, and for the rest of the time I was stressed, impatient, and angry. I had often heard that happiness was a choice. I felt it was time to find out if that was indeed true. I was tired of never feeling great without some external stimulus, alcohol, activity, etc.

I wanted to know if it was possible to be happy every day. Thanks to Anthony Robbins, a life strategist, I found out that happiness is just a state, and that you could instantly change your state. During this time, I also regularly listened to and applied the advice of sages, such as Mark Victor Hansen, Jack Canfield, Napoleon Hill, Robert G. Allen, Deepak Chopra, Oprah, and other well-known successful people.

I began to practice new techniques, such as meditation and visualisation, to bring into reality the life I had dreamed of. Most importantly, I discovered that it was possible to be happy in any moment of your life, and that happiness was really a choice.

I learned that you do not need external stimulants to be happy. Every day, I consciously decided to live in the emotions of happiness, gratitude, stress-free, ego-free, determined, passion, etc. I now believe that it is truly possible to design your life just as you imagined it. I have envisioned it and manifested it in my life, so I know it is possible for you.

I want to share with you the hope of that possibility for your lives. It is written in the Bible, "Seek and ye shall find"[8] (source). I dare you to look for yourselves. The answers are out there waiting for you to come looking and to ask with an open heart and mind.

Today, I finally live in the present. I appreciate where I am in my life and where I am headed in my future. You see, it was never about the place I lived or my role as a stay-at-home mom; it was always about my fears and my dreams. I may not know you intimately, but I know this: if you feel stuck, or if you feel that you have no more energy to achieve your dreams, then you are living in fear. I can also tell you that it is a horrible place to live, and I wish it on no one.

I almost gave up on my dreams. If I had, you would not be reading this book right now. Let me be your support, and let me be your light to find your path to this new beginning. Come with me, and we shall walk in peace together on this magnificent journey called life.

Take the time to explore what your life is worth. Only then can you stand up against the depletion of your humanity and your planet. True happiness will only come when we strive to become better human beings. We will bless others by fulfilling our true essence. Our personal happiness will help make the world a better place. We will inspire those around us to choose to live freer lives on their own terms.

The people who truly count are those who will love you no matter where your professional journey takes you. You don't have to let pride create artificial walls with those who love you. Let them in, because they

---

[8] Bible, John, Verses 4:3, translation *New King James Version.*

care nothing for your status and wealth. Make time to appreciate and cultivate those relationships. These relationships will be your source of strength when everything around you collapses.

Furthermore, learn to balance your life priorities. Begin to prepare financially for your new life by seeking knowledge from those who are already successful. This is the key to taking control of your life.

Do not build excessive debt by trying to prove your worth. Debt is the chain that keeps you under the feet of your corporate masters! You are perfect and worthwhile just because you are here on this earth, not because of what you possess.

I believe each of us has a unique role to play in the evolution of our world. The world is awaiting your contribution; it is literally a matter of life and death. If we do not find ways to fulfil our purpose, our dreams will die with us, and the world would have lost the opportunity to be enriched and blessed because you were here.

Most importantly, never allow the corporate environment to corrupt and destroy your humanity. Your legacy as a human being is all that remains in the passing of time.

Make it a priority to find ways to create the life you wish to live. Never rely on the money you earn to fulfil all of your needs. If you do so, one day you will find yourself alone with no real relationships to rely on.

STRESS ONLY HAPPENS WHEN YOU TAKE THINGS TOO PERSONALLY!

No doubt, stress is a new staple of the corporate environment. Stress is constantly with us, as we are continually pushed beyond our mental and physical capabilities by those in authority. There is so much to do with limited resources and too little time. Have you ever been in that predicament?

Unlike machines, we need downtime, relaxation, and enjoyment. Humans need appreciation, recognition, and skills training. As obvious as it sounds, it is quite common for companies to choose to ignore these needs and to continue to shovel work demands at employees.

Incessant demands cause employees additional mental anguish. Employees feel guilty for working on the weekends, but they are trapped. If they don't work, they will not only fail to deliver their quotas of work, but they will also lose all the things that they have toiled and sacrificed to amass. So, the only solution is to endure the stress and toil unendingly.

Work takes precedence over your family, your health, and sometimes your personal happiness. You become a slave worker, chained to the company with no way of redemption until the day you retire! That is your emancipation.

But stress only happens when you care too much about keeping your job. Instead, you need a paradigm shift to understand how to make corporates work for you, as discussed in chapter 8.

Finally, you may decide that the job is not for you but you like having the safety net of a pay cheque. So, instead of just walking out, you make a plan. You take time to see where you want to go, you find out what it takes to get there, you improve your skills and gain the necessary qualifications, you send out your CV/résumé, and then you only leave your current job when you have found the job you desire. In the meantime, you still provide your best service in your current job, reassured that you will soon find your dream job.

JOURNALING YOUR WAY TO SANITY

Initially, when I left or was kicked out of jobs because of one reason or the other, I would initially blame myself. I would expend energy focusing on my failures. As you can imagine, I became engrossed in massive pity parties.

After weeks of walking around in my pyjamas, I would get to the point when I became fed up with the blame game. At that point, I decided that

I had had enough. For most of my life I have chronicled my successes. It was only by re-living past successes that I found the courage to love myself and to feel worthy of success again. I hope this may help you to find your way too.

Buy a journal and write all of the great things about you. Write out all of your successes both small and large. Live in those moments and reaffirm how special and unique you truly are. Write out all of your strengths, and then list all of your weaknesses.

Finally make a plan to tackle all the areas you feel are weaknesses. Eventually, when people ask you what your weaknesses are, you can smile and confidently reply, "Well, I don't have any!" Just kidding, but I hope you get what I am trying to show you. We can turn any circumstances in our lives into a positive if we can be honest with ourselves and are willing to just put in the work.

My honest moment came when I realised that I was rubbish at some jobs, great at others, but never really in love with any of them. It was only when I did what came naturally to me—writing and speaking—that I re-ignited my passion for life and for living. Until then, I just drifted from one existence to the next, trading one country for another, one job for another, but never having any real purpose.

By moulding your mind and body into what you desire, you will gain great personal power and self-confidence. It takes you out of the clutches of the corporate talons. You become more valuable in your eyes and in the eyes of those around you. Your value is no longer determined by Human Resources departments or the job title they bestow on you. By living life on your terms, you free yourself from the bonds of corporate slavery.

COPING WITH LAYOFFS: MY MCI WORLDCOM STORY

Many people fear being laid off. In fact, some employees do whatever it takes to get out of the firing line. They may take a pay cut, create a security blanket of lies and deceit, and they may even sabotage their colleagues to make them look incompetent—anything to not get the axe. Finally, the inevitable happens whether we wish it or not.

In my career, I have been involved in three major layoffs. The worst one was when I worked for a great company called MCI, which was aggressively eaten up by WorldCom, and become known as MCIWorldcom. Yes, I was at the company for the Bernie Ebbers's corporate scandal.[9] At the time, Ebbers, the CEO of MCIWorldCom, was dominating Wall Street and he could do no wrong. Everyone wanted to invest in his companies. Ebbers built his empire through aggressive takeovers.

In the summer of 2002, MCIWorldCom declared bankruptcy due to an $11 billion accounting scandal. Ebbers and his cronies were accused of accounting fraud aimed at propping up MCIWorldCom's falling stock price. The scandal cost the company shareholders and employees billions of dollars in losses. According to the *Wall Street Journal*, "WorldCom's fraud and bankruptcy wiped out a stock that was worth more than $180 billion at its peak in 1999."[10] Ebbers, sixty-three, was convicted and received a life term for causing the downfall of MCIWorldCom.

Ebbers's conviction was of little comfort, because by the time the dust had settled, I had lost my entire 401k pension. All of my life's savings had evaporated! For years I had diligently put aside money for a rainy day. I had hoped, just as other WorldCom employees hoped, to become a millionaire by the time I retired.

My stock options were originally valued at approximately $200 per share prior to the takeover. Post-takeover and following my layoff, I would have actually had to pay to redeem my shares in the company.

---

[9] Ross Benson, "Lying, cheating cowboy and empire built on paper," *The Evening Standard*, April 12, 2012, http://www.standard.co.uk/news/lying-cheating-cowboy-and-empire-built-on-paper-6342812.html.

[10] Dionne Searcey, Shawn Young, and Kara Scannell, "Ebbers Is Sentenced to 25 Years For $11 Billion WorldCom Fraud," *The Wall Street Journal*, July 14, 2005, http://www.wsj.com/articles/SB112126001526184427.

During the layoff period, I saw people packing boxes and exiting the office. I noticed how those designated as the "in group" alienated those designated as the "out group." Senior managers who challenged the leadership of the new CEO were publicly whipped and shoved out of the business. This created a culture of "them versus us." We were often referred to by the new senior management team as "legacy MCIs." At lunch, everyone was afraid to speak against the new changes for fear that they would be reported and lose their jobs.

In this culture of fear, I still refused to betray my friends. The people who were laid off were perfectly competent, capable, and intelligent. Yet, in a mad twist of fate, they were treated quite the opposite. Many of the employees had been around since the inception of MCI and still shared fond memories of the old days. I enjoyed listening to how employees dived in with an entrepreneurial spirit and took the success of the company personally.

Having worked there for over five years before the takeover, I could see why the employees loved the company so much. The founders took care of their employees, and their employees took care of the company in return. The culture was amazing, and that was one of the reasons I worked so hard to join the company in the first place. I have never in my travels come across such a company, and if I ever did again I would offer to work there for free!

The layoffs didn't worry me. This was not because I did not have the usual bills like everyone else, but because I had been fortunate enough to meet one of the founders of the original MCI, who had long retired to his ranch in Texas. He came to see us in the midst of the takeover at a time when legacy MCI employees, as we were categorised, were deeply unhappy with MCIWorldCom's asset-stripping policies.

One day during a conference, our senior manager, who had been with the company in its formative years, noticed someone passing by the conference room. In mid-sentence, he ran out of the room and disappeared into the hallway. Everyone looked at each other wondering what had just happened. Another manager jokingly added that he probably needed to go to the bathroom. Everyone chuckled, but we all knew something else was amiss.

After a few minutes, the senior manager came back with a broad smile. He then warmly invited someone into the room. The man was unassuming, tall, and slim. He had kind eyes, and although not aloof, he had a certain authority about him. The senior manager smiled jubilantly at the team, hoping one of us would recognise the man who was standing quietly at the front of the room. We had no clue as to who he was. Finally, the senior manager introduced the man as one of the first partners of MCI and asked if he would share with us a nugget of wisdom.

The man smiled broadly. He asked how many of us knew about the history of the old company. People shouted out figures, growth rates, increasing market share, partnerships, and other performance-related information. The man gracefully accepted all of the responses. Then he told us of the days when the company was not a multimillion-dollar company.

He told us of the times when the company did not even have money to pay the engineers. In those days, he said the engineers opted to work for free because they enjoyed the work and had faith that the management would make good on their promises. Today, those very engineers were multimillionaires. Then he turned serious, as if something bothered him deeply, and when he spoke next, I suddenly understood why he had chosen to visit our company that day.

He said, "I am aware that the takeover of MCI really hurt the pride of the employees. I know that you, the workers, had been kept in the dark about the company's prospects by the board of directors. I know that if you were given the opportunity to help MCI you would have." He paused and scanned our reactions. He seemed to channel our feelings of disappointment and loss.

After a gap of silence, he continued. "I was just next door with the Research and Development team, and they informed me that they had projects on the backburner that could have saved the company, but the board had blocked all of their requests." He paused again.

It was as if he was endearing us to feel our anger and hurt, but in a controlled way. Finally he made a slight jump; it startled everyone in the room. When he had our full attention again, he spoke lovingly and with enormous sincerity. We all felt his attention and concern for us in his words.

He said, "Never mind about these things now. What you need to take from this experience is that you should be proud of the work you have done at the company. You should cherish the lifelong friendships you have cultivated. Hold your heads up high, because you were super employees and you embodied what MCI stood for. When they decide to remove you from the company, take it on the chin. You see, the new regime might try to strip us of everything by throwing us out of our beloved company and by taking away our livelihood, but they can never subdue our spirit and our sense of truth. They can never take away the fact that you are great employees who gave your best each day. Don't worry—other companies will see your worth and line up to hire you. The new bosses may trample on our values and tell us that the systems that we built from scratch are no good, but you know that is a lie. I thank you for being a part of MCI, and I know you all will be successful where ever you end up."

As abruptly as he had entered, he just as quickly left. Looking around the room, I could see that we all felt our spirits lifted.

Some weeks following our prep talk, a couple of things came true. Firstly, we all lost our jobs. Secondly, WorldCom tried to remove our bespoke systems but their systems soon crashed. It was not long before they had to revert to MCI's systems. Thirdly, many of the employees who were laid off were asked to return to work with the lure of higher salaries. Most of them refused to return. Fourthly, almost all of us were offered jobs with other firms within weeks of being laid off.

Other competitors saw hiring "legacy MCIs" as a chance to grab the talent they had previously lost to MCIWorldCom. Many of the new ideas that the engineers had created were adopted and utilised by the competitors who hired them. These companies used these ideas to take MCIWorldCom's market share. The world of work was never the same after that time, at least not in my eyes.

Finally, employees openly spoke up against asset-stripping and poor senior leadership of the company. Within weeks, those people were gone, but this time those who left were treated as comrades and not as lepers. We all held together to uplift each other. In the end we all had to leave, but we did so with our heads held high knowing that we did nothing wrong. It was the company's board that had let us down and they would eventually pay for destroying our company.

The lesson I learned that day helped me become immune to the idea of layoffs. I hope it will help you if you are ever in such a position. Never let them take your dignity. Never let them make you turn against your fellow colleagues. We are proud and moral people, and we work to the benefit of each other. So, if you feel that something is not in the best interest of the company that you helped build, don't be afraid to lift your head up and speak against it.

If you believe what you say to be true, then have the courage and the conviction to stand by it. If the management team is unprepared to consider your objections, then be prepared to leave the company. Never bow down and do things that are not good for your company no matter who demands it of you, and that includes the CEO him/herself.

ARE LAYOFF GAPS IMPORTANT?

In my former employment as an executive recruiter, I received many questions about whether having gaps in a CV or résumé would count against a candidate. My unreserved answer is NO! It is now commonplace for employees to get laid off. It is also commonplace for people to take time away from work. But it is your choice as to whether you want to disclose this information.

Everyone is looking for an opportunity to grow and to develop, and so it is expected that you might take time to find the next role that offers that opportunity of career progression. If you are struggling with gaps, look at the section on becoming a "core worker" in chapter 9, because when you live in this space, gaps become irrelevant.

Having been a stay-at-home mom for a number of years, I have a six-year gap in my CV/résumé with regard to corporate work. However, I did work on both my networking and recruitment businesses during that time, so I have that listed. If you have done charity work or helped out with some small projects, list those briefly in the gaps.

Alternatively, just note that you took a sabbatical. But do take one. Then have an interesting story to tell about that time. Maybe you can transport your interviewers to a time when you visited some exotic place and the lessons you learned, which were relevant to the role you are applying for. Or perhaps you took time to do some charity work. Organisations with high ethical codes of conduct like to hire those with similar values.

Today, I get the calls when there is no one else to fill the role. I get the call when they need such diverse skill sets and there are only a handful of people who have them. This is the space you want to occupy. This is the position where you can control the price of your labour and gaps don't ever factor into the equation. Naturally, I turn these roles down because I am here to serve you and to campaign to protect our planet.

CHAPTER 7

You ALWAYS Have a Choice

The strongest principle of growth lies in human choice
George Eliot

I stumbled through life and work trying to find the right place for me. Mainly, I was led by work opportunities and survival rather than what was aligned with my inner desires and talents. I found this to be the case with many of my fellow employees as well. It is truly rare to find individuals who love their jobs and wake up each morning with a spring in their step.

I spent many years trying to discover if there was indeed a better way. I desperately wanted to be like the few who hummed their way to work, were anxious to solve the next challenge, and confident that they would be recognised and rewarded for their ingenuity.

PUTTING THINGS INTO PERSPECTIVE

For most of us, the stress and fear of being unemployed is enough to keep us hitched to the wagon. For others, the fear of losing all of our possessions or our status with friends and family is enough to keep us tied to the hamster wheel. Whatever the reason for staying in work, you must always be clear about why you are there, where you are heading, and what it would take for you to achieve personal self-fulfilment.

It is not enough to wake up each morning and put on your work mask. It is not acceptable to spend most of your life unhappily toiling in a job you hate, watching your life swiftly pass you by. If you are on this road, I hope you will also find the courage to pause and reflect on your life and the choices you have made.

WOLVES ARE THE PERPETRATORS OF CORPORATE FRAUD

While many people believe that the collapse of the global economy in 2007/2008 was the fault of a few unscrupulous individuals, this is not the case. A closer look would reveal that it was a manufactured bubble and hundreds of wolves were in on it. Many investors knew of the financial collapse years before it happened. Some investors made tidy profits as hard-working people lost their livelihoods. The people who knew refused to raise the alarm in the years leading up to the financial collapse.

Money and greed drove their silence. Sadly, the people who knew about the impending danger continue to be some of the richest people in our society. I suppose there is never a limit on greed, and it seems that even one's conscience can be bought for a price. Human tragedy is just a brief nuisance in the wealth-making schemes of wolves.

When high-level crimes are perpetrated, it is not the guilty who suffer but the underlings—the common people who can only accept the fate meted to them by financial institutions and government organisations. I love capitalism and I believe that people deserve all that they work for.

However, we are in desperate need of an investment in humanity. We need to be working toward a healthy society with strong family values and a level of wellness that is standard for all human beings. What's ironic is that this desire is achievable in this very moment, yet it has not been made a priority by our leaders.

SHOULD I STAY OR SHOULD I GO?

If you choose to stay in a job that is killing you, then you must take responsibility for the consequences: loss of creativity, depression, stress, etc. If you choose to leave the job, then you must face the consequences: unemployment, poverty, loss of status, etc.

The great thing about life is that nothing is as clear-cut as those two options; there are grey areas in between. You may leave your job; feel better for doing so, then feel depressed while struggling to find another job. But then you may find a job you are completely happy with.

Alternatively, you may choose to stay in your occupation but look at it in a new way. Changing your perspective of why you are there will help to relieve stress and keep you from depression. You will not fight battles not worth fighting, or worry excessively about things not working at its best. All you have to do is to provide a fair day's work for your agreed wages.

NOT ENOUGH TIME!

If there never seems to be enough time to do it all, then you need to focus on what is most important and give it priority over all else. In the extra moments, you can fix the less-important things. Understand what tools you are working with and your limitations. Don't be afraid to ask for help.

It's hard to be a great mother and a sole breadwinner. It's hard to be an energetic father when your last conversation was with your boss at five on a Friday evening insisting that a critical piece of work needs to be completed by Monday morning at nine, which effectively means that you will be working on the weekend. Something has to give!

Unfortunately, what you choose to sacrifice is the easiest to give away, but that which was once lost can never be regained. You can lose fortunes and make them back much more than before, but the time lost with your family is gone forever. Yet, you make this sacrifice without too much of a fight by rationalising that it is necessary for your family's survival.

You are caught between a rock and a hard place. You must work to provide shelter and to put food on the table. In the midst of all of that, you also know that bread alone will never feed the soul and your soul feels empty. It is only during your irregular sleep patterns that you find some solace from the cross you have to bear each day.

I think the "what-if" game is a good way of planning your next move. I am not referring to leaving your job; it is about thinking what your life would be like *if*. It gives me great comfort when I find bits of my life that I would do all over again in a heartbeat. I am also saddened to find that there are not as many moments as I had hoped for.

The good news is that each day provides a new beginning. In each day is a new opportunity, a new chance to have an amazing time and to share amazing moments. These moments are the gems that will fill your soul.

I know it can be difficult when you are standing on a crowded underground train, with no one making eye contact, and everyone is pretending to be more important than the other person. I know what it's like when someone spills coffee on your neatly pressed white shirt while you are on your way to close a deal you have been working on day and night for the last three months. I suppose life is not so rosy, and maybe all of the other people on the train are feeling this pressure too.

It is no wonder that we lose our way in the confusion of life. Our lives are devoid of the joy of living, the beauty in simplicity, or any gratitude for all that we have. But don't worry, because the feelings of gratitude and joy can be cultivated daily. No matter what situation you are in, if you able to force yourself to think positively about your situation, the clouds will part and eventually blue skies will appear. You see, no matter what you are going through, you can be sure that you are not the only one experiencing this.

Believe this! There are people who have travelled the very road you are on and have managed to find the light at the end of the tunnel. Seek out those people, learn from them, and your life will become better. By taking the time to read this book, you have vastly increased your chances of having an amazing life. The only thing left to do now is to act decisively on your goals and enjoy the journey as you come to experience your own greatness.

DON'T FALL INTO THE BLAME GAME

Never blame anyone for the choices you make. It is always easy to blame your husband, your wife, your boss, and your circumstances for not having the life you wish for yourself. Don't toil under the illusion that you are enduring this wretched state for your family. Never believe the lie that you are doing what's best for your family by enduring poor treatment and terrible work conditions. When you hurt, your family hurts. The more you hurt, the more they hurt.

Your happiness is just as important to your family as having nice, luxurious things. A family that loves and supports you will be willing to give up all the tea in China to see you happy and healthy.

Sometimes we may have to work for corporates even if only for a short time. Working for corporates can be quite rewarding financially and emotionally. If you are lucky to work for one of the few companies that take a genuinely benevolent approach to its employees, you will enjoy your work life immensely.

On other occasions, you may be forced to work for corporates for mere survival. You will need to pay your bills and take care of your family. This is okay too. If you want to grow a business, it would probably be a good idea to work for a similar type of company to learn how you can do a better job and win key accounts. This purpose is different from just irking out an existence.

Finding out the reason why you need to work for corporates is important. If you need to feel that sense of fraternity, then keep looking and building your skills until you find a company that is worthy of your time and life energies.

CHAPTER 8

The New Paradigm of Work—
Core Workers' Rule

I have been impressed with the urgency of doing.
Knowing is not enough; we must apply.
Being willing is not enough; we must do.

Leonardo da Vinci

You need to be aware of when your work world is changing around you. You need to understand your role in the organisation. You need to know why you are there. Then you need to make a game plan on how you can become an indispensable part of the core capability of the company.

LIONHEARTS ARE VALUED FOR THEIR SKILLS

To end the cycle of corporate time stealing and still work for corporates you need to make yourselves invaluable. This means you have to find skills that are in demand and become completely competent in them. The more difficult the skill is to learn, the more money corporates will pay you to acquire them. You need to upgrade your intellectual capital. The good news is that corporates cannot take your intellectual capital from you when you leave!

This approach will benefit both you and your company because you will become more capable, thereby increasing the capability of the firm. Additionally, you will make yourself indispensable and a valued member of the workforce.

Should your company decide that they no longer need your services, you can easily walk into another role. No longer would you have the stress of worrying about restructures and layoffs. If you want to move, there are many other companies that are willing to pay top money for your skills.

LEARNING SHOULD BE AN INTEGRAL PART OF LIVING

The best way to ensure that you always stay ahead of the layoff curve is to become indispensable. You will need to be willing to challenge yourself and to sacrifice time to upgrade your skills. Learning needs to become an integral part of your working life.

Take advantage of all the resources your employer has on offer. Plot your map on where you are and what skills you need to acquire. Keep abreast of the external economic forces, develop a relationship with recruiters in your field, and find out what skills are in high demand and what skills companies pay top money for. Make a plan to cultivate those skills, preferably at the expense of your employer.

CHAPTER 9

Finding Alternative Ways to Make a Living

People are always blaming their circumstances for what they are.

I don't believe in circumstances. The people who get on in this world are the people, who get up and look for the circumstances they want, and if they can't find them, make them.

George Bernard Shaw

One of the ways we can move beyond the corporate bollocks is to tap into the theory of abundance. You can choose to believe that life is limitless and there is unlimited opportunity in the world. Some people may struggle to grasp this metaphysical concept, but just go with it. You have nothing to lose but everything to gain.

ABUNDANT OPPORTUNITIES

There is an abundance of ways for you to make money. You just cannot choose to sit where you are, never doing anything differently, and expect different results. Others don't change, circumstances don't change, and your life won't change until YOU change. Knowing this is a powerful key to opening your door to opportunity.

There are many ways you can approach this change, but all change requires action. The first method is a short-term fix but guarantees you the safety of finding a job. The second and third options are more long-term. All paths require planning, soul searching, and commitment. All of these methods are pathways for survival and making a good living, but they are not the only ways. If you would take time to explore your great creative genius, I am certain you can find a path that is unique and rewarding just for you!

PATHWAY 1: BECOMING A CORE EMPLOYEE

A core employee is someone whose skills are essential to the profitability of the company. Heated battles are fought between corporations for the services of core employees; they are the crème de la crème of the workforce. As such, senior management vigorously protects the wellbeing of core employees from office power politics, as well as ring fencing their massive budgetary allowances from cost-cutting reviews.

The way to become a core employee is to look at the skills or professions that are in short supply, high demand, or are difficult to learn. If you have the time, motivation, and perseverance, you can retrain in this field. Your job would be almost guaranteed.

Retraining does not necessarily mean going to college to complete a four-year degree course. However, you can also choose to gain a diploma in your chosen field. This would provide you with the practical skills necessary to quickly get started in your new profession. Internships are another good way of gaining essential experience. Don't worry about age; it is about your determination and goals.

PATHWAY 2: ENTREPRENEURISM

This pathway is the most fearful, can take a little longer, but it is extremely rewarding. Entrepreneurism is also not for everyone. You have to be happy spending hours working on your business and be open to calculated risk-taking. Therefore, it is essential to do something that you love so that when the going gets tough you will stick with it until you achieve your desired results.

It is worth reading about your favourite entrepreneurs. You will find that they are not as superior as you may think. In fact, they are not too different from you and me. Many entrepreneurs started from humble beginnings. You might even find that you actually have more resources at your disposal right now than they had when they started their businesses. The main difference between you and these entrepreneurs is that they reinforced their self-belief with each success, big and small.

Building a personal diary of success, no matter how small, will help you to develop the self-belief you need to pursue your dreams. You can start with simple things like managing to eat healthy, taking time to exercise, or taking time to read one book a week about someone you admire. Whatever it is, make sure that it contributes to where you want to end up in life and the person you dream of becoming. Each step taken brings you farther out of the hole you are stuck in and closer to your dream of freedom.

PATHWAY 3: ASPIRATIONAL EMPLOYMENT

This pathway is my favourite, because the goal is to live each day and enjoy your life. The term "aspirational employment" means that you are working to fulfil your goals that are beyond your basic survival needs such as working to create a revolution in conscious consumerism. Achieving aspirational employment leads to self-actualisation, which is participating in something greater than one's self.

You may not be too surprised to learn that life is much more enjoyable at the top. I think most people know this, but few actually know that their daily activities are constantly sabotaging their chances of ever reaching that rarefied space.

That is why it is so important to "forget the corporate bollocks"; if you don't, you will be destined to a life of mediocrity. You will never get to aspirational employment if all your energies are focused on fighting battles in the corporate jungle.

There are many good books out there to guide you to find your true purpose in life: *Man's Search for Meaning* by Viktor Frankl or *Think and*

Grow Rich by Napoleon Hill. Additionally, you can invest in yourself and hire a life coach. Life coaches are available from Anthony Robbins, Earl Nightingale, or Deepak Chopra. Their coaches and products are dedicated to helping you find your true path. You don't have to wait until you retire! If you don't want to spend any money then go to the library. You can borrow autobiographies and personal development books. This will give you a head start in your new life and inspire you to keep going even when things get tough.

When you find your true vocation, the darkness will be lifted. You will love whatever you do so much that it will be as easy as breathing. You will have purpose, you will feel energised each day, and you will hop out of bed happy to get started on your work ahead.

Your life will be inspired and you will connect with the present. You will live in the moment and happiness will be plentiful. This path is more difficult because it requires a leap of faith; you will be guided by a higher purpose.

To gain entry to this pathway, you will have to take time away to re-think your existence. You will need to have something substantial to give up. You may need to work for a few years to save to get to this point. Your first mighty challenge would be to cut away from your existing life and to deal with feeling fearful. However, if you are committed to your journey, you will find the courage to move past the fear and end up on the other side. Sometimes your journey may take you to distant lands in search of yourself and your history.

This journey cannot be completed half-heartedly. Once started, you will no longer be able to continue lying to yourself that everything is okay. You will have to face the honesty of your situation, your untamed desires, and your unrealised dreams. Here is where you start building your dream life. Search deep inside to find out what you are passionate about. Be willing to let go and just go for it!

These paths are not exhaustive; there are endless opportunities for you to manifest your greatness on earth. You just need to take time away from the corporate world to find those paths. This is why layoffs can actually be a blessing in disguise. As long as you are tied to a job, you will find excuses to not work on yourself. Once the yolk has been lifted, you are free to contemplate your own existence.

If you are still at work, then seeking your true path may require just taking a few minutes at lunch or after work just for yourself. In that quiet moment, just focus on asking yourself a few simple questions: "What is it I really want?" "What does my heart truly desire?" "What would make me feel the greatest joy?" Listen with your heart, accept, and act on your received answers.

I hope you take the time to work on yourself and to find your true path. Only then will you be able to help me in my mission to save our planet. You see, only when you rise out of your ashes can you then notice the world around you. When this happens, you can become a major influencer in the revolution in conscious consumerism. It is only first by changing yourself that the world around you changes too.

CHAPTER 10

Rebalancing the Scales of Capitalism

*It is not the critic who counts; not the man who
points out how the strong man stumbles, or where
the doer of deeds could have done them better.
The credit belongs to the man who is actually in
the arena, whose face is marred by dust and sweat
and blood . . . who at the best knows in the end the
triumph of high achievement and who at the worst,
if he fails, at least he fails while daring greatly. So
that his place shall never be with those cold and
timid souls who know neither victory nor defeat.*

Theodore Roosevelt,
26th President of the United States

There is a building-block approach to rebalancing the scales of capitalism. On an individual level, conscious consumerism will create a tiny rip in the capitalist fabric. The actions of each individual bundled together will create a collective avalanche, collective consumerism, that will tilt the scales permanently on the side of the consumer.

CONSCIOUS CONSUMERISM

Conscious consumerism means just taking a few minutes, at the point of sale, to quickly consider the total cost of products and services. By making informed purchase decisions we can drive home the idea of planetary sustainability.

When we need to buy new things, we need to consider the actual cost of these products: the environmental and human cost. It is only then that we will become conscious consumers, and only then will we be able to develop leverage over companies to put our planet and human beings in front of profitability. It all starts with each conscious decision to only buy products that are of high quality and sustainable. Refusal to buy products from companies who have been continuously caught misleading consumers will spur more positive corporate behaviours.

There are many websites devoted to helping you understand the idea of conscious consumerism. One of my favourite sites is Newdream.[11] This organisation is dedicated to improving well-being based on the way we consume. The individuals who are a part of that organisation are solid in their commitment and they would be happy to welcome you as a volunteer.

Another organisation that has a strong message about conscious consumerism and offers amazing support is to our well-being is All Things Healing (ATH).[12] Additionally, if you are motivated to do more, you might want to create your very own website to promote the idea of conscious consumerism. Effort multiplied is the best way to change any system.

COLLECTIVE CONSUMERISM

The next step to build momentum is to tell others about what you have discovered and get them to act as well. Then, as you educate your family and friends, a little expression of will evolves into a massive shift in consumer spending. With mobile Internet technology at our fingertips, we can easily share research on what we are buying, and this will have a tremendous butterfly effect. Just as a butterfly spreads life through its wings, your small purchase decisions will energise the revolution in conscious consumerism.

Only by harnessing the machine of collective consumerism will we be able to regain our collective working dignity, halt the destruction of our humanity, and save our planet. There are some very unscrupulous

---

[11] New Dream, https://www.newdream.org/programs/beyond-consumerism/rethinking-stuff/conscious-consumerism.
[12] All Things Healing, http://www.allthingshealing.com/conscious-consumerism-definition.php#.Vjyq8p8nzDd.

people running the very companies you work for, and if you think for a moment that you will come in the way of their profitability, think again! We need to build leverage.

BE THE CAUSE!

Whether you are aware of it or not, you are contributing to destruction of the world. I know this might be a bit uncomfortable for you to hear. The large institutional investors are driven and empowered by you. When you invest in companies that demand profitability at all costs, you infect the capitalist machine with greed.

Your pension pot is invested somewhere, but do you know where? I hope you will find out. Most large investment institutions invest in the very companies you work in. What this means is that you are driven to achieve profits to help build your pension pots. No issue there, right?

Well, this is a problem if your company translates institutional demands into a rotten culture and demoralising middle and upper management— you will be responsible for creating your very own work hell! We can remedy this situation by taking time to see where our money is invested and what corporate behaviours it is driving. It is extremely important for you to understand the vicious cycle of consumerism.

The Vicious Cycle of Consumerism

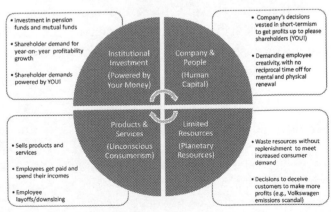

- Investment in pension funds and mutual funds
- Shareholder demand for year-on-year profitability growth
- Shareholder demands powered by YOU!

Institutional Investment (Powered by Your Money)

- Company's decisions vested in short-termism to get profits up to please shareholders (YOU!)
- Demanding employee creativity, with no reciprocal time off for mental and physical renewal

Company & People (Human Capital)

Products & Services (Unconscious Consumerism)

- Sells products and services
- Employees get paid and spend their incomes
- Employee layoffs/downsizing

Limited Resources (Planetary Resources)

- Waste resources without replenishment to meet increased consumer demand
- Decisions to deceive customers to make more profits (e.g., Volkswagen emissions scandal)

Publicly traded corporates are owned by institutional investors who demand year-on-year profit at any cost. Here is the kicker: YOU are the people these institutional investors represent. Your pension and investment pots give them the power to drive demands for year-on-year profitability. These corporates respond to this pressure by draining their employees of their life energies. You are at the top and bottom of the cycle. If you chose to spend some time to understand your contribution to the cycle, you can do your bit to alleviate the plight of your fellow workers.

RECLAIMING OUR DIGNITY

Workers all over the world are experiencing that very same sense of loneliness in thoughts and meekness in action in their work lives. We need to take back our collective work dignity, to save our planet, and to protect our future. It is not difficult for you to help; with a little action from each individual, we, the global masses, will rebalance the scales of capitalism.

This book begins the conversation to stemming the tide of the destruction of our lives, our families, and our planet by those who would unscrupulously see us replaced with machines to increase profits. There are those who think they control us when in fact it is us, humans, who hold the key through our consumerism.

Working together can rebalance the scales of capitalism and make it work for the enrichment of our world. However, this can only be done by working simultaneously on an individual level as well as on a collective level.

REVERSING PLANETARY CHAOS

What will we do when our planet is destroyed and turned to ash? Who gets to start a new life in space? Would it be those who profited and destroyed our planet, or the poor global workers?

Does it not matter that only the rich will survive in the new world after we have destroyed our planet? They would be the only ones who could afford to buy their places on-board the spaceships. This is quite ironic, since it will be their unscrupulous wealth creation methods that will destroy our planet and humankind.

Where do you fit in this cycle? Are you just going to sit back and watch it unfold? What about the future of your family? Too many times, you say, "I need to work to feed my family and to survive. Protecting the environment is for those eco-warriors or someone else, definitely not me. I am only one person!"

We always have choices. We can either chose to do something or chose to do nothing. So, what can we do? We all need to work and earn a living, right? We offer our time and companies offer a salary in return. That's okay. It is wonderful to work and to contribute to society. However, it is essential that you recognise the difference between working for a livelihood and becoming a trapped worker bee.

Banded together, we can become a force to be reckoned with. I hope you will join me on this journey to reclaim our collective humanity and to save our planet. I have put together some steps to help us get started on our journey.

STEP 1: GETTING THE WORD OUT

We must band together and educate ourselves about what is happening around us. We must also recognise that we are part of the problem *and* the solution. We have to all work together to halt this monster we have collectively created.

The machine is always going to look too big for one person to tackle. In fact, if one person tried to stop a major corporate bulldozer, it would be career suicide. So here is the alternative: we work under the water to help disrupt these corporates by making conscious purchasing choices.

By anonymously sharing information about poor treatment and unstainable practices, we can publicly shame these companies. It is my wish that we shame them into walking the straight and narrow. We need to spread the word about unethical practices, so that they can be nipped in the bud. We need to use this information to force the hand of change in these corporates.

We can use the very technology that keeps us tethered to our jobs as a freedom tool. It is important to shame corporations for their unscrupulous behaviours and appalling treatment of their staff. Your verified contributions, anonymous or not, will help to provide the impetus for us to approach the directors of companies or governments to change and to correct the issues burdening global employees.

STEP 2: LEG ACTION

We can make a massive change in the way capitalism functions if we take time to educate ourselves about the way companies do business. Demand that investments of our pensions only be in companies that have their acts together. This will be a massive step to correcting this faulty system.

If you find out that your money is invested in companies that have been flaunting their disregard for environmental legislation, then you can choose to withdraw your money. It is important to tell these institutional investment companies about the behaviours you want to encourage when you choose to invest your hard-earned cash. You will also be protecting your future wealth, because only companies that treat their employees with dignity and respect will survive in the new era of business.

STEP 3: BECOMING A COLLECTIVE CONSUMER

As a collective consumer, it would be your responsibility to only support companies whose behaviours are positive for both global employees and the environment. As consumers, we need to actively support corporates that have a history of replenishing the environment.

We will be looking for corporates that have outstanding environmental records. We should favour corporates that are open to listening to their local communities. Look at papers put out by academics whose research is not funded by major corporates.

If corporates fail to heed calls to make REAL change, they will not have a future in the new era of accountability and world citizenship. These old dinosaurs will become extinct in the new revolutionised world order. We, the collective consumers, will make sure this happens.

CHAPTER 11

Corporate Social Responsibility (CSR)

> *"Good people do not need laws to tell them to act responsibly, while bad people will find a way around the laws."*
>
> Plato
> *(427–347 BC)*

C orporation Social Responsibly (CSR) means that corporates recognise that they are an integral part of the communities they serve. They understand that poor management decisions, such as a plant closure, can have detrimental effects on these communities. In light of this, corporates willingly accept and acknowledge that they have a responsibility to the people they employ and the communities they do business with. Unfortunately, for some corporations, CSR has become the new buzz phrase for pretending to care about the communities they destroy with their greed.

CORPORATE SOCIAL RESPONSIBILITY (CSR): A PR EXERCISE

These unethical corporates are not a part of your communities; they only give back if it is in their best interest to do so. Many companies claim corporate social responsibility (CSR), but it is only a fad to get you to think that they care. If they did care, they would make environmental accounting a major part of their financial process. They would pay for their usage of our natural resources, and they would be held accountable by governments for replenishing these resources.

Unfortunately, no one will hold these corporates accountable because they are the key contributors to governments. Their monies put only those in office who willingly support their cause. The question then becomes, who speaks for YOU?

Don't be so naïve to think the answer lies with the trade unions. Many trade unions are political machines. Some seek to amass more and more power but do little to help you achieve the work dignity you deserve. Some unions work so closely with corporates that they become intertwined with the strategy of the company and have little desire to challenge them on your behalf.

Other companies have been lucky enough to get rid of trade unions altogether; this means that you have to rely on Human Resources or an external tribunal to fight your battles. Here again, you face an uphill battle and most employees just end up signing compromise agreements and disappearing into the night.

By working together, we can become the controllers of our own destinies. We are actually one community of global citizens. When we strive together, we not only make the world a better place, but we pick up little gems of happiness along the way. We will succeed in regaining our collective humanity and protecting our planet through collective consumerism and environmental accountability programs.

CHAPTER 12

Environmental Accountability

Human history becomes more and more a
race between education and catastrophe.

H. G. Wells

I t is time we demand some accountability and payment for fixing all of the ills corporates have begotten from their end-to-end supply chain. There must be a cost associated with the usage of our limited planetary resources. This type of accountability will temper corporates' forecasts for profit making. It will also hold corporates accountable for pollution and the degradation of our human capital.

CORPORATE DESTRUCTION OF OUR PLANET

Many corporates turn a blind eye to the destruction of our planet and our human capital. Incidentally, there is no global monitoring body to hold them accountable for their actions. Therefore, instead of using our limited planetary resources to the benefit of all, corporates use it to further their own self-interest.

These unscrupulous companies have politicians and governments in the palms of their hands. These corporates amass unlimited power through global consolidations. As their monopoly over natural resources grows, they can exert more influence on global governments.[13]

---

[13] David C. Korten, "Do Corporations Rule the World? And does it Matter?", *Organization & Environment* 11, no. 4 (1998): 389–398.

Corporates can then influence governments to pass policies that make countries more favourable for them to conduct business. This is done with little consideration for the welfare of global workers.

In 2014, a BBC investigative report by Richard Bilton highlighted the poor working conditions in China at Foxconn, Apple's biggest components supplier. According to the report, "rules on workers' hours, ID cards, dormitories, work meetings and juvenile workers were routinely breached."[14] Ironically, in 2010, fourteen workers from this same factory committed suicide. According to the BBC program, Apple refused to acknowledge any issues regarding safe working practices at the supplier site. Richard Bilton also worked on a BBC special on Apple's failure to abide by its promise to customers.[15] Apple claimed that it was dedicated to ethically sourcing materials, but it was revealed that they were not fulfilling this promise.

The BBC program reported on the existence of illegal mines providing tin, which was fed into Apple's supply chain. The BBC team reported that children were digging tin ore out by hand. As expected, Apple once again declined to provide any public comment.

By raising these ethical issues, companies like Apple, could begin to pay more attention to their supply chains and take adequate corrective actions. Consequently, in an email to Apple's staff from their senior vice president of operations, Jeff Williams, this pledge was included: "We will not rest until every person in our supply chain is treated with the respect and dignity they deserve."[16]

We have limited resources on our planet, and if we don't insist that corporations balance resource usage with replenishment, our earth will soon be unable to sustain us. We live in a greed-driven society,

[14] Richard Bilton, "Apple failing to protect Chinese factory workers," *BBC Panorama*, December 18, 2014, http://www.bbc.co.uk/news/business-30532463.
[15] Richard Bilton, "Apple 'deeply offended' by BBC investigation," *BBC Panorama*, December 19, 2014, http://www.bbc.co.uk/news/technology-30548468.
[16] Richard Bilton, "Apple 'deeply offended' by BBC investigation," *BBC Panorama*, December 19, 2014, http://www.bbc.co.uk/news/technology-30548468.

and man's greedy nature is rapidly using up more resources without equally replenishing them. Research supports that we are using up 30 percent more natural resources than we can replenish annually.[17] We are creating an ecological disaster beyond the financial crisis in 2007/2008. The world is dying. We are facing deforestation, polluted air and water, declines in the populations of all living species (i.e., fish, turtles, rhinos, lions, etc.), and the list goes on.

To help change the world, you only need to make small changes in your daily life. One of the best ways to do your bit for the world is to get your finances under control. Live with less if you need to, but choose good stuff. Did you know that purchasing cheaply produced things made by unskilled child labourers is not actually a saving?

I have owned expensive shoes for almost a decade and they are still worth something. We spend a lot of money on rubbish, which we toss out because it is easily broken or destroyed. If you were to spend a little extra in the right places, you would find that you would have actually saved yourself a great deal of money in the longer term. Things made with love and true qualities tend to last for decades.

You can help to keep our planet sustainable. Buy well-made products from companies that run their businesses with integrity and that put aside a portion of their profits for charity. Find out from employees how they are treated. Choose to spend your money at companies that reward their employees and are committed by their actions to replenishing our limited planetary resources.

We need to ensure that we are connected to the truth—not the stories handpicked by the media, but from reputable sources who value their reputation above their salaries. Learn the truth from journalists who still believe that journalistic integrity cannot be bought for any price.

---

[17] Juliette Jowit, "World is facing a natural resources crisis worse than financial crunch," *The Guardian*, October 29, 2008, http://www.theguardian.com/environment/2008/oct/29/climatechange-endangeredhabitats.

They are few, but they are out there working for you. Let's offer them our respect and support.

Finally, when you learn the truth, share it with others. This will force governments to act sternly against corporates who willingly deceive their customers. By making a public example of these dishonest corporates, other corporates will be foolish to think of tricking or lying to us again.

These little shifts in consumer spending can catapult our capitalist society into a more balanced and caring one. If businesses continually refuse to behave ethically and to produce products sustainably, customers should drive them out of existence by boycotting their products.

MANDATORY ENVIRONMENTAL ACCOUNTING SYSTEM

We can stem the tide of corporate greed by demanding that governments across the globe mandate a system of environmental accounting. These submissions should be made alongside the usual financial accounting statements, such as profit and loss balance sheets.

WHY ARE OUR PLANETARY RESOURCES FREE?

Many corporations utilise resources, including human capital, to produce products and services. Therefore, they should have a responsibility to replenish those resources through sustainability studies and project funding, research and development, renewable energy employee training, employee well-being programs (i.e. shorter work week, flexible work hours, environmental regeneration programs (i.e. tree planting, etc.)).

World governments should work with corporates to create centres of learning for skill development in areas of renewable energies. There should be encouragement to create learner-friendly curriculums that meet the needs of the three generations in work.

Government investment and employee training programs aimed at renewable energies would create new jobs and develop a future for the renewable energy industry. Renewable energy is harnessed from natural resources such as the sun, wind, and water. It enables our energy stores to be naturally replenished. For instance, more investment should be made in training people to work in companies harnessing tidal, wave, and photovoltaic (PV) solar energy options for electricity.

Geothermal energy[18] can be considered for heating homes. Some countries, such as Kenya and Costa Rica, generate more than 15 percent of their electricity from this cost-effective, environmentally friendly energy source.

We have allowed some unscrupulous corporations to use and abuse our planet for too long. These moneymaking machines have become rich at our expense. They have polluted our environment and reduced our global citizens to worker bees. There are many organisations you can join to gain knowledge and to help the world.

One of my favourite sites is the Union of Concerned Scientist (UCS). This society has been around for a long time and has been involved in many ways to keep our environment safe. For example, UCS plays a "key role in passing landmark emissions and fuel efficiency standards that will cut in half the global warming emissions of new cars and light trucks by 2025."[19]

ABOLISHMENT OF CARBON EMISSIONS TRADING

Companies should be held accountable and tasked with maintaining a harmonious eco-system. If companies are unable to hit carbon targets

---

[18] Ingvar B. Fridleifsson et al, "The possible role and contribution of geothermal energy to the mitigation of climate change," *In IPCC scoping meeting on renewable energy sources, proceedings*, Luebeck, Germany, vol. 20, no. 25, pp. 59–80, 2008.
[19] Union of Concerned Scientist (UCS), http://www.ucsusa.org/.

and other environmental safety regulations, they should revise their profitability forecast and use the money to invest in research and development projects.

If a company cannot meet their carbon emissions quotas, they should downgrade their businesses and focus on what they can manage to produce without breaking the legal limits.

Trading carbon emissions does not stop polluters from destroying the environment. If there are companies below their carbon emissions quotas, then these should be revised to reflect what those companies could reasonably achieve, and it should be continuous process to get better and better at protecting the environment.

CHARITIES INVOLVED IN BREAKING THE CYCLE!

There are global charities that understand that the cycle can only be broken by us, the consumers. They know that it is all tied to financial markets and choices made by institutional investors. These people make choices for YOU. They decide where your pensions and other investment monies go.

You can take control of who invests your money and in what companies. We need to work together to name and shame corporates that abuse their employees and destroy our planet. We can make them accountable by simply controlling where we choose to bank and what funds we invest our future incomes for retirement.

This might seem overwhelming to most, so there are charities set up to help you.

Here are some websites to get started:

> Research about various companies' end-to-end moneymaking processes:
> www.enhanced-analytics.com

➤ Fair Pensions Campaign: Launched by Amnesty International, Green- peace, Oxfam, and WWF. Looks into where pensions are invested and how these companies impact the world: www.fairpensions.org.uk

I look forward to taking this journey with you and to seeing our world become a better and more humane place. I look forward to delivering a world worth inheriting to our future generations.

WORKS CITED

All Things Healing. "Conscious Consumerism." October 18, 2015. http://
www.allthingshealing.com/conscious-consumerism-definition.
php#.Vjyq8p8nzDd (accessed October 18, 2015).

Association, Press. "John West accused of breaking tuna pledge to end
destructive fishing methods." *The Guardian.* October 6, 2015.
http://www.theguardian.com/environment/2015/oct/06/john-
west-accused-of-breaking-tuna-pledge-to-end-destructive-
fishing-methods. (accessed October 6, 2015).

Benson, Ross. "Lying, cheating cowboy and empire built on paper."
The Evening Standard. April 12, 2012. http://www.standard.
co.uk/news/lying-cheating -cowboy-and-empire-built-on-
paper-6342812.html (accessed September 15, 2015).

Bilton, Richard. "Apple deeply offended by BBC investigation." Ceri
Thomas. December 19, 2014. http://www.bbc.co.uk/news/
technology-30548468.

—. "Apple failing to protect Chinese factory workers." BBC
Panorama. December 18, 2014. http://www.bbc.co.uk/news/
business 30532463.

Bloomberg. "Following the FIFA Fiasco." *Bloomberg News.* July 17,
2015. http://www.bloomberg. com/graphics/2015-fifa-scandal
(accessed July 17, 2015).

Cervantes Saavedra, Miguel,. *El ingenioso hidalgo Don Quijote de la
Mancha.* Colección, 1999.

Eliot, George. *The George Eliot Letters: 1852-1858.* Vol. 2. Yale University
Press, 1954.

Frankl, Viktor Emil. *Man's Search for Meaning.* Simon and Schuster, 1985.

Fridleifsson, Ingvar B., Ruggero Bertani, Ernst Huenges, John W. Lund, Arni Ragnarsson, and Ladislaus Rybach. "The possible role and contribution of geothermal energy to the mitigation of climate change." *IPCC scoping meeting on renewable energy sources, proceedings.* Germany: IPCC, 2008. 59–80.

Goldblatt, David. "The Fifa fiasco proves it's time to dismantle football's edifice of corruption." May 27, 2015. http://www.theguardian.com/commentisfree /2015/may/27/fifa-fiasco-football-corruption.

Gordon, Rayner. "Adolf Merckle: what made this German billionaire commit suicide." *The Telegraph* . January 9, 2009. http://www.telegraph.co.uk/finance/recession/4210246/Adolf-Merckle-what-made-this-German-billionaire-commit-suicide.html. (accessed October 7, 2015).

Hutten, Russell. "Volkswagen." October 28, 2015. http://www.bbc.co.uk/news/business-34324772 (accessed October 28, 2015).

Jowit, Juliette. "World is facing a natural resources crisis worse than financial crunch." *The Guardian.* London, October 29, 2008.

Korten, David C. "Do Corporations Rule the World? And does it Matter?" *Environment and Organization* 11, no. no.4 (1998): 389-398.

New Dream. "Beyond Consumerism." October 18, 2015. https://www.newdream.org/programs/beyond-consumerism/ rethinking-stuff/conscious-consumerism (accessed October 18, 2015).

Phelps, Edmund S. "Short-termism is undermining America." *New Perspectives Quarterly*, October 28, 2010: 17-19.

Roosevelt, Theodore. 1858–1919 & 1901–1909.

Searcey, Dionne, Shawn, Young, and Kara, Scannell. "Ebbers is sentenced to 25 years for $11 Billion WorldCom fraud." *The Wall Street Journal.* July 14, 2005. http://www.wsj.com/articles/ SB112126001526184427 (accessed October 2, 2015).

Shaw, George Bernard. 1856–1950.

Smith, Adam. 1723–1790.

—. *The wealth of nations.* [1776]. na, 1937.

Union of Concerned Scientist. *On the Front Lines of Climate Change.* November 23, 2015. (accessed November 23, 2015).

Vinci, Leonardo da. 1452–1519.

Wells, H. G. 1866–1946.

ACKNOWLEDGEMENTS

To those I love, thank you for your unending unconditional love and support.

ABOUT THE AUTHOR

CAMILLE WORDSWORTH was born on Tobago, a tiny Caribbean island. Camille attended university in the United States to pursue a business degree.

Over the course of her career specialising in marketing and finance, she has lived in the United States, the Caribbean, and Europe; consequently, she has a deep affinity to the plight of global workers.

At forty years old, Camille went back to university to pursue her master's degree. Camille holds a master's degree in business and advanced accounting qualifications.

Camille witnessed first-hand how tough job layoffs and restructures were on employees, and she knew from experience how stressful these situations can be. Camille was driven to light a path for others to follow.

After spending decades working for many large corporations, Camille focused on using her knowledge to find a way to help those who felt trapped in their jobs and performing unfulfilling work.

Camille has a global perspective when it comes to work and the planet. She hopes to show the world how truly similar we all are in our desire for justice, fair treatment, and to protect our planet.

Printed in the United States
by Baker & Taylor Publisher Services